WINDSWEPT
collection one

to

Mark, for your love and constant support

Mum and Dad, wish you were still here

CONTENTS

Page

8 DESIGNS
   A collection of contemporary fairisle and cable garments

38 GALLERY
   An easy reference tool for the collection

40 PATTERNS
   Instructions needed to make each design

73 INFORMATION
   All the information needed for each design including
   any techniques, finishing and button details

75 CREDITS
   Thank you's

WINDSWEPT

......is a celebration of traditional fairisle and cable patterning with a hint of crochet.

The modern and classic fit garments are perfect to wear at home or on bracing

country or seaside walks and look great styled with tartans and plaids. The collection

shows my love of colourwork and detailing with some of the designs having optional

crochet trimmings. These added embellishments make the garments unique, but of

course it's your choice if you add them or not! The designs are knitted using some

of my favourite Rowan yarns, including Felted Tweed, Rowan Fine Tweed and Cocoon

- the beautiful colours and rustic textures of these yarns complimenting the

traditional nature of my patterns perfectly.

I hope that you will enjoy knitting from my first exclusive collection.

Marie
X

Thyme
Wrap

Lovage

Camomile
Tam

Oak
Scarf

Dill

Comfrey

Comfrey

Sage

Leaf
Waistcoat

Rosemary

Rosemary

Parsley

Parsley

30

Willow

Mint
Wrap

Mint Wrap

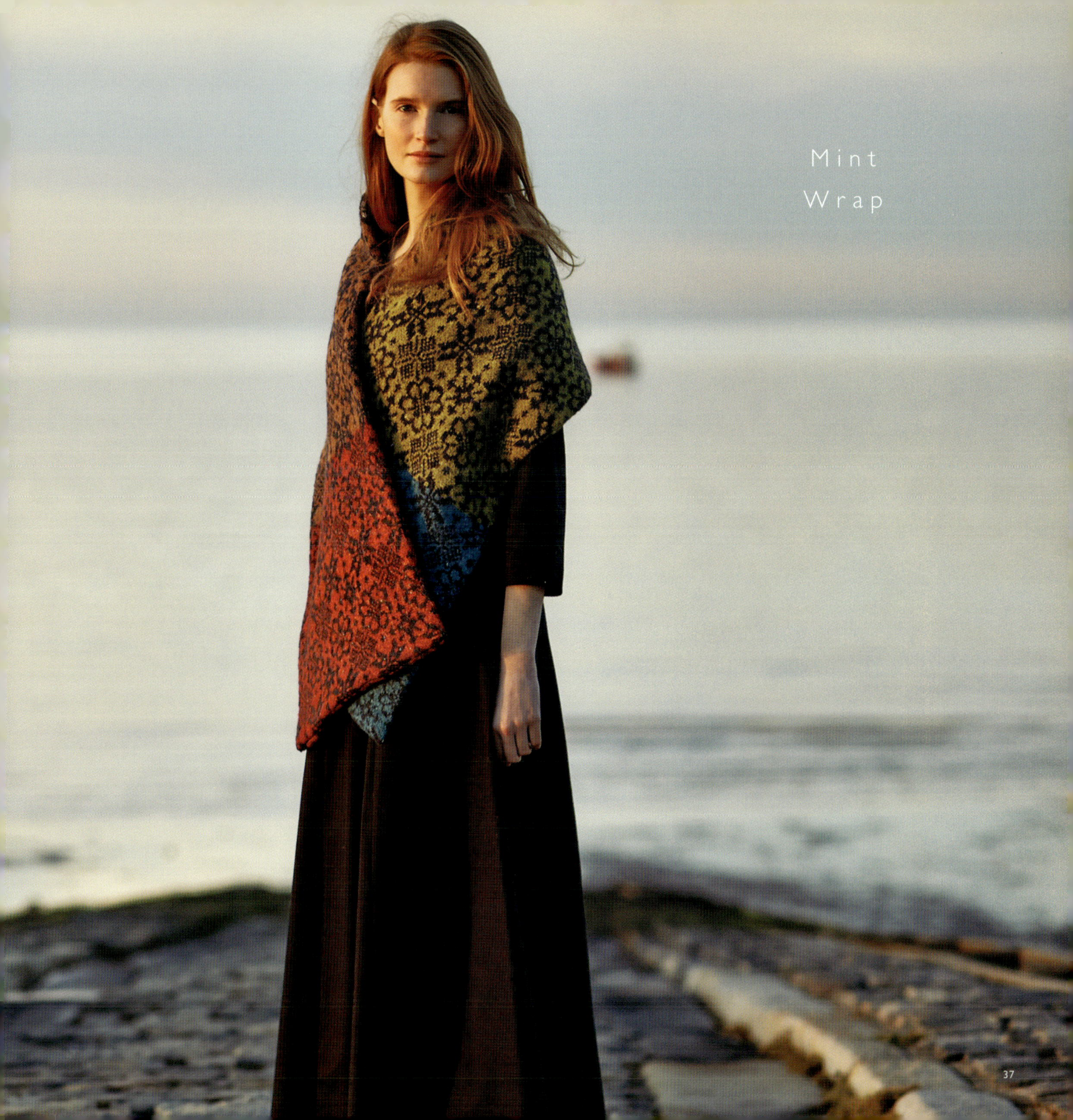

GALLERY

THYME WRAP
Main image pages 6, 7, 8, & 9
Pattern page 58

LOVAGE
Main image pages 10 & 11
Pattern page 64

CAMOMILE TAM
Main image pages 12
Pattern page 44

OAK SCARF
Main image pages 5 & 13
Pattern page 72

DILL
Main image pages 14 & 15
Pattern page 45

COMFREY
Main image pages 16, 17, 18 & 19
Pattern page 61

SAGE
Main image pages 20 & 21
Pattern page 40

LEAF WAISTCOAT
Main image pages 22, 23 & 39
Pattern page 47

PARSLEY
Main image pages 28, 29, 30, 31 & 39
Pattern page 51

ROSEMARY
Main image pages 24, 25, 26 & 27
Pattern page 55

WILLOW
Main image pages 32 & 33
Pattern page 68

MINT WRAP
Main image pages 34, 35, 36 & 37
Pattern page 60

SAGE ● ● ●

	S	M	L	XL	XXL	
To fit bust	81-86	91-97	102-107	112-117	122-127	cm
	32-34	36-38	40-42	44-46	48-50	in

Rowan Felted Tweed

		S	M	L	XL	XXL	
A	Clay 177	2	3	3	3	4	x 50gm
B	Phantom 153	2	2	3	2	3	x 50gm
C	Hedgerow 187	2	2	2	2	2	x 50gm
D	Gilt 160	2	2	2	3	3	x 50gm
E	Maritime 167	1	1	1	1	2	x 50gm
F	Ginger 154	1	1	1	1	1	x 50gm
G	Cinnamon 175	1	1	1	1	2	x 50gm
H	Bilberry 151	1	1	1	1	1	x 50gm
I	Peony 183	1	1	1	2	2	x 50gm
J	Avocado 161	1	1	1	1	1	x 50gm
K	Watery 152	1	1	1	2	2	x 50gm
L	Tawny 186	1	1	1	1	2	x 50gm
M	Camel 157	1	1	1	2	2	x 50gm

Needles

1 pair 2¾mm (no 12) (US 2) needles
1 pair 3¼mm (no 10) (US 3) needles

Tension

29 sts and 30 rows to 10 cm measured over patterned st st using 3¼mm (US 3) needles.

BACK

Using 2¾mm (US 2) needles and yarn A cast on 157 [171: 189: 207: 227] sts.
Row 1 (RS): K1, *P1, K1, rep from * to end.
Row 2: P1, *K1, P1, rep from * to end.
Join in yarn B.
Keeping yarn not in use at **WS** of work (this is back of work on RS rows, and front of work on WS rows), cont as folls:
Row 3: Using yarn A K1, *using yarn B P1, using yarn A K1, rep from * to end.
Row 4: Using yarn A P1, *using yarn B K1, using yarn A P1, rep from * to end.
Rows 5 to 16: As rows 3 and 4, 6 times.
Break off yarn B and cont using yarn A **only**.
Rows 17 and 18: As rows 1 and 2.
Change to 3¼mm (US 3) needles.
Beg and ending rows as indicated, using the **fairisle** technique as described on the information page and repeating the 88 row patt repeat throughout, cont in patt from chart, which is worked entirely in st st beg with a K row, as folls:
Work 24 rows, ending with RS facing for next row.**
Keeping patt correct, dec 1 st at each end of next and foll 8th row, then on 3 foll 6th rows, then on 10 foll 4th rows. 127 [141: 159: 177: 197] sts.
***Work 21 [21: 23: 23: 25] rows, ending with RS facing for next row.
Inc 1 st at each end of next and 2 foll 16th rows, taking inc sts into patt. 133 [147: 165: 183: 203] sts.
Cont straight until back meas 57 [58: 59: 60: 61] cm, ending with RS facing for next row.

Shape armholes

Keeping patt correct, cast off 3 [5: 7: 9: 11] sts at beg of next 2 rows. 127 [137: 151: 165: 181] sts.
Dec 1 st at each end of next 5 [7: 9: 11: 13] rows, then on foll 3 [3: 4: 5: 6] alt rows. 111 [117: 125: 133: 143] sts.

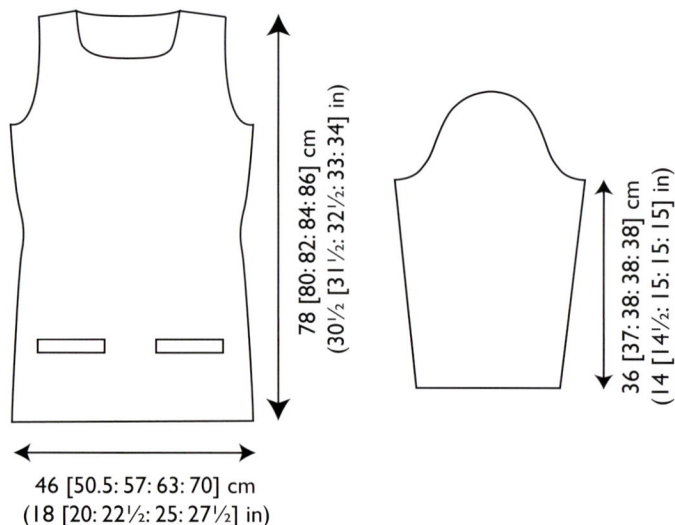

78 [80: 82: 84: 86] cm
(30½ [31½: 32½: 33: 34] in)

46 [50.5: 57: 63: 70] cm
(18 [20: 22½: 25: 27½] in)

36 [37: 38: 38: 38] cm
(14 [14½: 15: 15: 15] in)

Cont straight until armhole meas 17.5 [18.5: 19.5: 20.5: 21.5] cm, ending with RS facing for next row.
Shape back neck
Next row (RS): Patt 23 [26: 29: 33: 37] sts and turn, leaving rem sts on a holder.
Work each side of neck separately.
Dec 1 st at neck edge of next 6 rows. 17 [20: 23: 27: 31] sts.
Work 1 row, ending with RS facing for next row.
Shape shoulder
Cast off 5 [6: 7: 8: 10] sts at beg and dec 1 st at end of next row.
Work 1 row.
Rep last 2 rows once more.
Cast off rem 5 [6: 7: 9: 9] sts.
With RS facing, slip centre 65 [65: 67: 67: 69] sts onto a holder, rejoin yarns and patt to end.
Complete to match first side, reversing shapings.

POCKET LININGS (make 2)
Using 3¼mm (US 3) needles and yarn A cast on 35 [35: 37: 37: 39] sts.
Beg with a K row, work in st st for 52 rows, ending with RS facing for next row.
Next row (RS): K3 [3: 4: 4: 5], M1, (K4, M1) 7 times, K4 [4: 5: 5: 6].
43 [43: 45: 45: 47] sts.
Break yarn and leave sts on a holder.

FRONT
Work as given for back to **.
Keeping patt correct, dec 1 st at each end of next and foll 8th row, then on 3 foll 6th rows, ending with **WS** facing for next row.
147 [161: 179: 197: 217] sts.
Place pockets
Next row (WS): Patt 15 [17: 19: 21: 23] sts, slip next 43 [43: 45: 45: 47] sts onto a holder and, in their place, patt across 43 [43: 45: 45: 47] sts of first pocket lining, patt 31 [41: 51: 65: 77] sts, slip next 43 [43: 45: 45: 47] sts onto a holder and, in their place, patt across 43 [43: 45: 45: 47] sts of second pocket lining, patt 15 [17: 19: 21: 23] sts.
Cont in patt, dec 1 st at each end of 3rd and 9 foll 4th rows.
127 [141: 159: 177: 197] sts.
Now work as given for back from *** until 20 [20: 22: 22: 24] rows less have been worked than on back to beg of shoulder shaping, ending with RS facing for next row.
Shape front neck
Next row (RS): Patt 28 [31: 35: 39: 44] sts and turn, leaving rem sts on a holder.
Work each side of neck separately.
Keeping patt correct, dec 1 st at neck edge of next 10 rows, then on foll 2 [2: 3: 3: 4] alt rows, then on foll 4th row. 15 [18: 21: 25: 29] sts.
Work 1 row, ending with RS facing for next row.
Shape shoulder
Cast off 5 [6: 7: 8: 10] sts at beg of next and foll alt row.
Work 1 row.
Cast off rem 5 [6: 7: 9: 9] sts.
With RS facing, slip centre 55 sts onto a holder, rejoin yarns and patt to end.

Complete to match first side, reversing shapings.

SLEEVES
Using 2¾mm (US 2) needles and yarn A cast on 69 [73: 75: 75: 79] sts.
Row 1 (RS): K1, *P1, K1, rep from * to end.
Row 2: P1, *K1, P1, rep from * to end.
Join in yarn B.
Keeping yarn not in use at **WS** of work (this is back of work on RS rows, and front of work on WS rows), cont as folls:
Row 3: Using yarn A K1, *using yarn B P1, using yarn A K1, rep from * to end.
Row 4: Using yarn A P1, *using yarn B K1, using yarn A P1, rep from * to end.
Last 2 rows set the sts.
Cont as now set, inc 1 st at each end of next and 1 [1: 2: 2: 2] foll 6th [6th: 4th: 4th: 4th] rows, taking inc sts into patt. 73 [77: 81: 81: 85] sts.
Work a further 5 [5: 3: 3: 3] rows, ending with RS facing for next row.
Break off yarn B and cont using yarn A **only**.
Row 17 (RS): Inc in first st, K0 [0: 1: 1: 1], *P1, K1, rep from * to last 2 [2: 1: 1: 1] sts, P1 [1: 0: 0: 0], inc in last st. 75 [79: 83: 83: 87] sts.
Row 18: P0 [0: 1: 1: 1], *K1, P1, rep from * to last 1 [1: 0: 0: 0] st, K1 [1: 0: 0: 0].
Change to 3¼mm (US 3) needles.
Beg and ending rows as indicated, cont in patt from chart as folls:
Inc 1 st at each end of 5th [5th: 5th: 3rd: 3rd] and every foll 6th [6th: 6th: 4th: 4th] row to 93 [101: 111: 101: 111] sts, then on every foll 8th [8th: -: 6th: 6th] row until there are 99 [105: -: 117: 123] sts, taking inc sts into patt.
Cont straight until sleeve meas 36 [37: 38: 38: 38] cm, ending with RS facing for next row.
Shape top
Keeping patt correct, cast off 3 [5: 7: 9: 11] sts at beg of next 2 rows. 93 [95: 97: 99: 101] sts.
Dec 1 st at each end of next 11 rows, then on every foll alt row until 53 sts rem, then on foll 7 rows, ending with RS facing for next row. 39 sts.
Cast off 4 sts at beg of next 4 rows.
Cast off rem 23 sts.

MAKING UP
Press as described on the information page.
Join right shoulder seam using back stitch, or mattress stitch if preferred.
Neckband
With RS facing, using 2¾mm (US 2) needles and yarn A, pick up and knit 20 [20: 22: 22: 24] sts down left side of front neck, K across 55 sts on front holder, pick up and knit 20 [20: 22: 22: 24] sts up right side of front neck, and 11 sts down right side of back neck, K across 65 [65: 67: 67: 69] sts on back holder dec 1 st at centre, then pick up and knit 11 sts up left side of back neck. 181 [181: 187: 187: 193] sts.
Row 1 (WS): P1, *K1, P1, rep from * to end.
Join in yarn B.
Keeping yarn not in use at **WS** of work (this is back of work on RS rows, and front of work on WS rows), cont as folls:
Row 2: Using yarn A K1, *using yarn B P1, using yarn A K1, rep from * to end.

Row 3: Using yarn A P1, *using yarn B K1, using yarn A P1, rep from * to end.
Rows 4 to 7: As rows 2 and 3, twice.
Break off yarn B and cont using yarn A **only**.
Row 8: K1, *P1, K1, rep from * to end.
Row 9: As row 2.
Cast off in rib.

Pocket tops (both alike)
Slip 43 [43: 45: 45: 47] sts from pocket holder onto 2¾mm (US 2) needles and rejoin yarn A with RS facing.
Row 1 (RS): Knit.
Row 2: K1, *P1, K1, rep from * to end.
Join in yarn B.
Keeping yarn not in use at **WS** of work (this is back of work on RS rows,

KEY

□ A. Clay 177

✕ B. Phantom 153

○ C. Hedgerow 187

╲ D. Gilt 160

• E. Maritime 167

▼ F. Ginger 154

■ G. Cinnamon 175

– H. Bilberry 151

△ I. Peony 183

● J. Avocado 161

⋀ K. Watery 152

◿ L. Tawny 186

╱ M. Camel 157

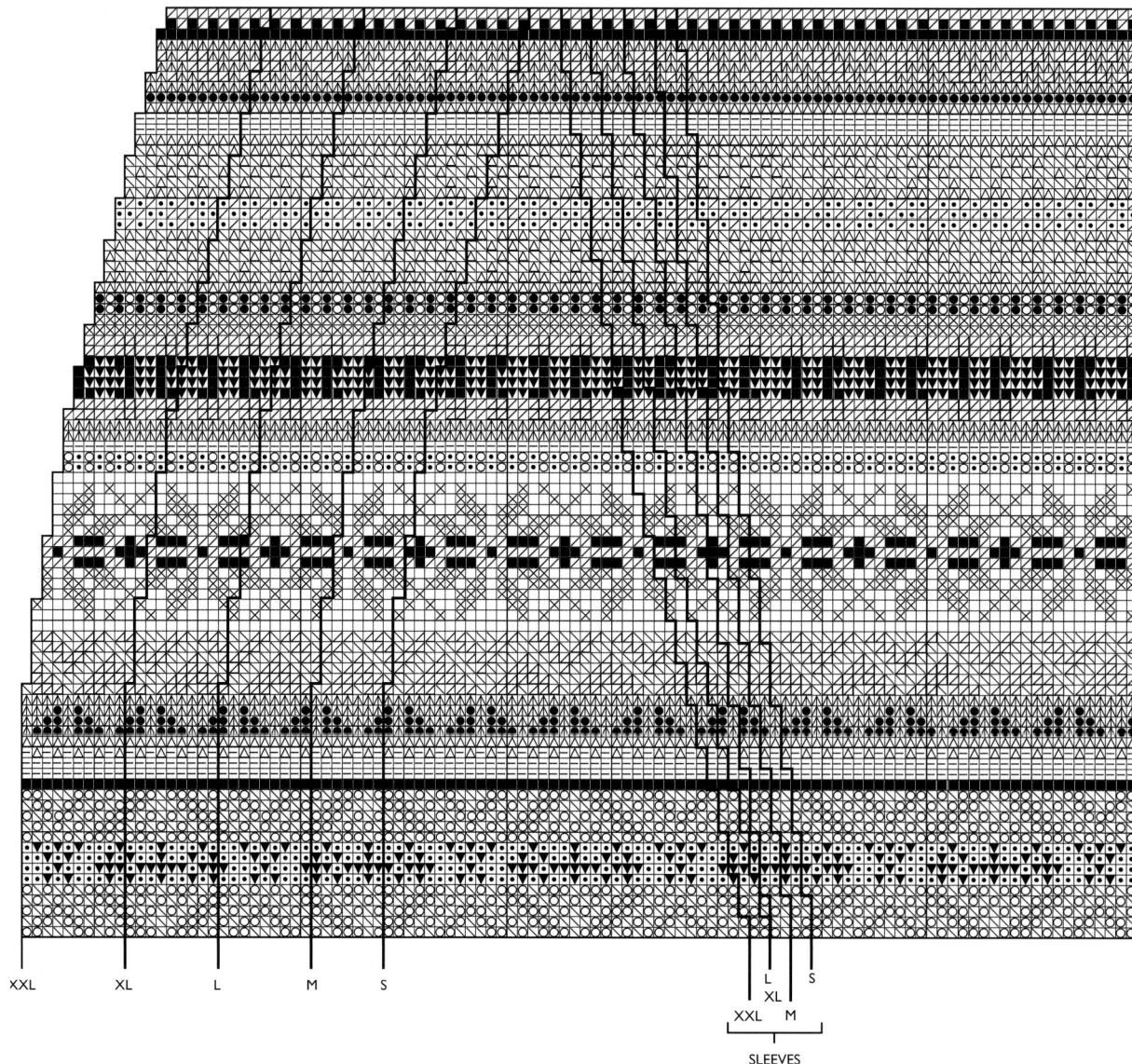

XXL   XL   L   M   S

L
XXL XL
XXL M   S

SLEEVES

42

and front of work on WS rows), cont as folls:

Row 3: Using yarn A K2, *using yarn B P1, using yarn A K1, rep from * to last st, using yarn A K1.

Row 4: Using yarn A K1, P1, *using yarn B K1, using yarn A P1, rep from * to last st, using yarn A K1.

Rows 5 and 6: As rows 3 and 4.

Break off yarn B and cont using yarn A **only**.

Row 7: K2, *P1, K1, rep from * to last st, K1.

Row 8: As row 2.

Cast off in rib.

See information page for finishing instructions, setting in sleeves using the set-in method. Sew pocket linings in place on inside, then neatly sew down ends of pocket tops.

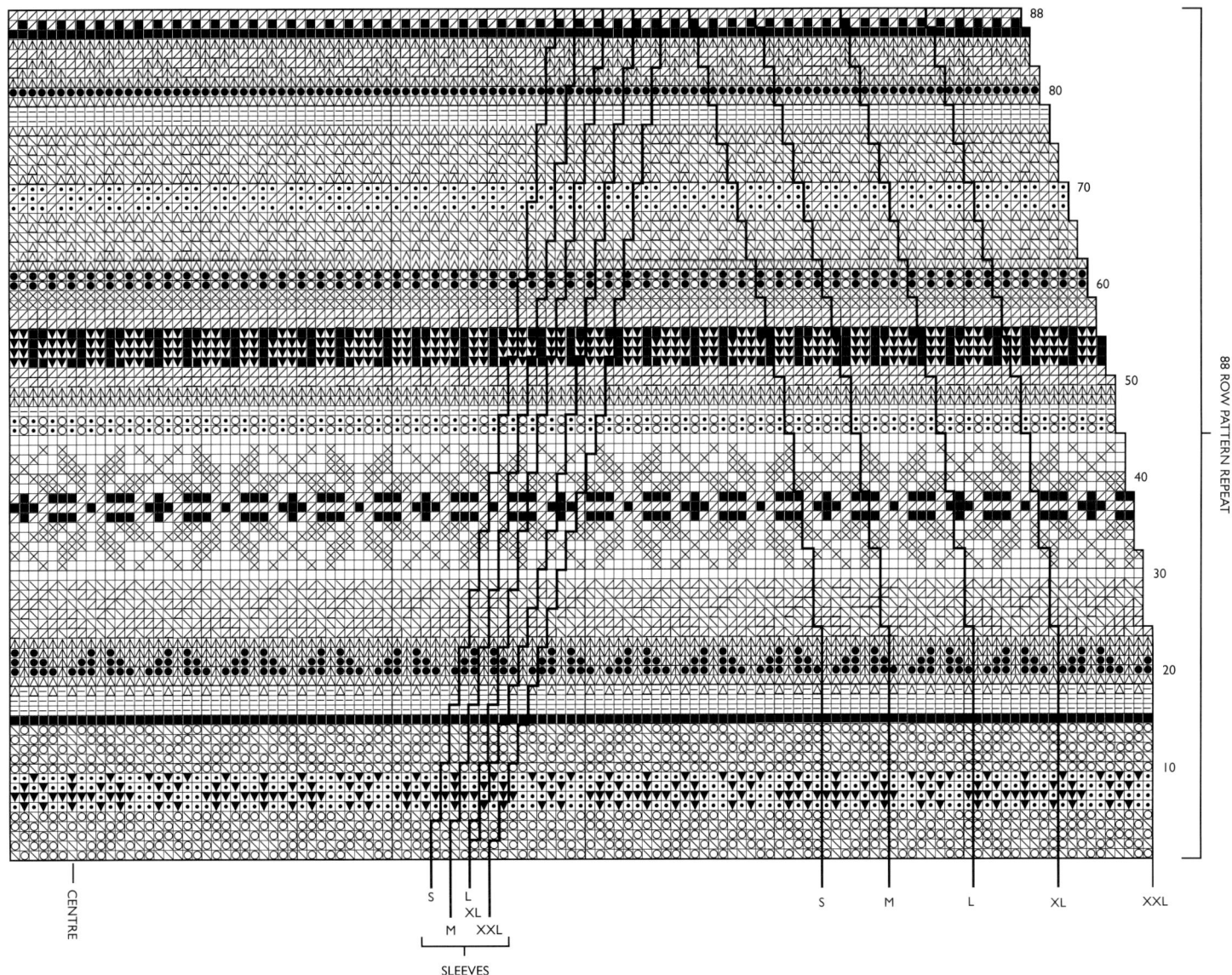

88 ROW PATTERN REPEAT

CENTRE

SLEEVES

S M L XL XXL

S M L XL XXL

Round 2: As round 1.
Rep rounds 1 and 2 until brim measures 3cm from cast on edge.
Break off yarn A.
Change to 3¼mm (US 3) circular needles.

Work sides and crown of tam
Round 1: Using yarn B, K1, *M1, K2; rep from * to last st, M1, K1. 168 sts. Beg and ending rounds as indicated, using the **fairisle** technique as described on the information page and repeating the marked 24 st rep (7 times in total), cont in patt from chart starting at round 2 of chart, which is worked entirely in st st in the round. Cont to work from the chart until row 56 has been completed, working decreases as indicated on the following rounds:
Round 35: (Patt 10 sts, K2tog tbl, K2tog, patt 10 sts) 7 times. 154 sts.
Round 37: (Patt 9 sts, K2tog tbl, K2tog, patt 9 sts) 7 times. 140 sts.
Round 39: (Patt 8 sts, K2tog tbl, K2tog, patt 8 sts) 7 times. 126 sts.
Round 41: (Patt 7 sts, K2tog tbl, K2tog, patt 7 sts) 7 times. 112 sts.

KEY

A	□	Camel 157	E	•	Bilberry 151
B	✕	Hedgerow 187	F	△	Tawny 186
C	■	Avocado 161	G	∣	Cinnamon 175
D	○	Ginger 154			

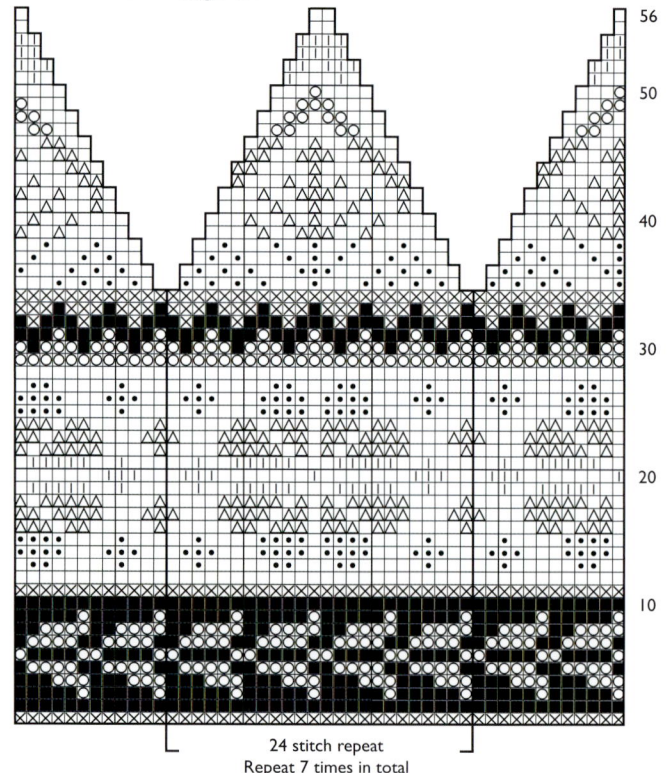

24 stitch repeat
Repeat 7 times in total

CAMOMILE TAM ●●

One size only
To fit average head
53 – 56cm (21 – 22in)

Rowan Felted Tweed

A	Camel 157	1	× 50gm
B	Hedgerow 187	1	× 50gm
C	Avocado 161	1	× 50gm
D	Ginger 154	1	× 50gm
E	Bilberry 151	1	× 50gm
F	Tawny 186	1	× 50gm
G	Cinnamon 175	1	× 50gm

Needles
2¾mm (no 12) (US 2) circular needle
3¼mm (no 10) (US 3) circular needle

Tension
28 sts and 30 rounds to 10 cm measured over patterned st st using 3¼mm (US 3) needles.

TAM
Brim
Using 2¾mm (US 2) circular needles and yarn A, cast on 112 sts.
Round 1: *K2, P2; rep from * to end of round.

Round 43: (Patt 6 sts, K2tog tbl, K2tog, patt 6 sts) 7 times. 98 sts.
Round 45: (Patt 5 sts, K2tog tbl, K2tog, patt 5 sts) 7 times. 84 sts.
Round 47: (Patt 4 sts, K2tog tbl, K2tog, patt 4 sts) 7 times. 70 sts.
Round 49: (Patt 3 sts, K2tog tbl, K2tog, patt 3 sts) 7 times. 56 sts.
Round 51: (Patt 2 sts, K2tog tbl, K2tog, patt 2 sts) 7 times. 42 sts.
Round 53: (Patt 1 st, K2tog tbl, K2tog, patt 1 st) 7 times. 28 sts.
Round 55: (K2tog tbl, K2tog) 7 times. 14 sts.

Next round: Using yarn A, (K2 tog) 7 times. 7 sts.
Break off yarn and draw up tightly.

FINISHING
Fasten off centre of tam to WS.
Weave in any loose ends to WS of tam.
Press the tam gently on the WS using a warm iron over a damp cloth.

Cable needle
2.50mm (no 12) (US C2) crochet hook (optional)

Tension
15 sts and 20 rows to 10 cm measured over st st, 18 sts and 20 rows to 10 cm measured over sleeve patt, both using 6mm (US 10) needles.

Special abbreviations
C2B = slip next st onto cable needle and leave at back of work, K1, then K1 from cable needle; **C2F** = slip next st onto cable needle and leave at front of work, K1, then K1 from cable needle; **Cr2L** = slip next st onto cable needle and leave at front of work, P1, then K1 from cable needle; **Cr2R** = slip next st onto cable needle and leave at back of work, K1, then P1 from cable needle.

Crochet abbreviations
ch = chain; **dc** = double crochet; **sp(s)** = space(s); **tr** = treble.
See information page for US abbreviations.

BACK
Using 6mm (US 10) needles cast on 66 [74: 82: 92: 102] sts.
Work in g st for 2 rows, ending with RS facing for next row.
Beg with a K row, now work in st st throughout as folls:
Work 10 [12: 12: 14: 14] rows, ending with RS facing for next row.
Next row (RS): K3, sl 1, K1, psso, K to last 5 sts, K2tog, K3.
Working all side seam decreases as set by last row, dec 1 st at each end

DILL ●●

To fit bust	S	M	L	XL	XXL	
	81-86	91-97	102-107	112-117	122-127	cm
	32-34	36-38	40-42	44-46	48-50	in
Rowan Cocoon						
	6	6	7	7	8	x 100gm
*Rowan Fine Tweed	1	1	1	1	1	x 25gm

*One ball of Rowan Fine Tweed for optional crochet neck trim (photographed in Cocoon in Alpine 802 with crochet trim in Rowan Fine Tweed in Buckden 364)

Needles
1 pair 6mm (no 4) (US 10) needles

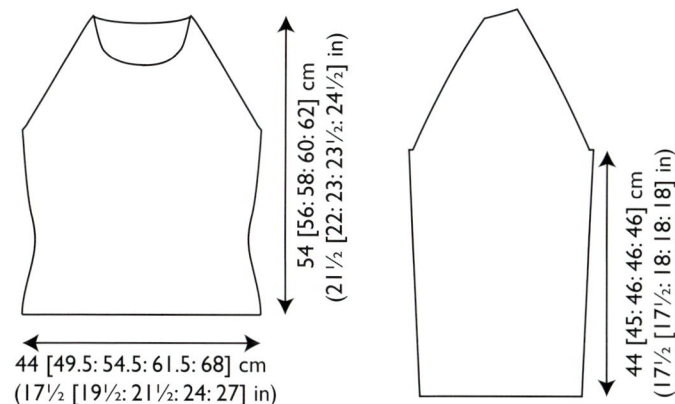

54 [56: 58: 60: 62] cm
(21½ [22: 23: 23½: 24½] in)

44 [49.5: 54.5: 61.5: 68] cm
(17½ [19½: 21½: 24: 27] in)

44 [45: 46: 46: 46] cm
(17½ [17½: 18: 18: 18] in)

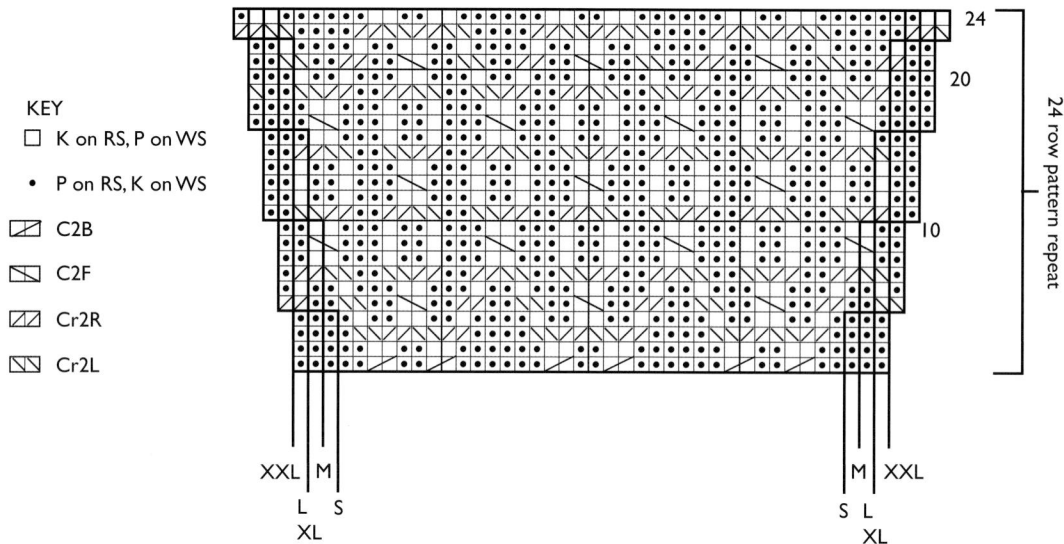

KEY

☐ K on RS, P on WS

• P on RS, K on WS

⬛ C2B

⬛ C2F

⬛ Cr2R

⬛ Cr2L

of 6th and foll 6th row. 60 [68: 76: 86: 96] sts.
Work 13 rows, ending with RS facing for next row.
Next row (RS): K3, M1, K to last 3 sts, M1, K3.
Working all side seam increases as set by last row, inc 1 st at each end of 10th and foll 10th row. 66 [74: 82: 92: 102] sts.
Cont straight until back meas 34 [35: 36: 37: 38] cm, ending with RS facing for next row.

Shape raglan armholes

Cast off 3 sts at beg of next 2 rows. 60 [68: 76: 86: 96] sts.
Next row (RS): K3, sl 1, K1, psso, K to last 5 sts, K2tog, K3.
Next row: (P3, P2tog) 0 [1: 1: 1: 1] times, P to last 0 [5: 5: 5: 5] sts, (P2tog tbl, P3) 0 [1: 1: 1: 1] times.
Working all raglan armhole decreases as set by last 2 rows, dec 1 st at each end of next 1 [5: 9: 17: 23] rows, then on foll 15 [14: 13: 10: 8] alt rows. 26 [26: 28: 28: 30] sts.
Work 1 row, ending with RS facing for next row.
Break yarn and leave sts on a holder.

FRONT

Work as given for back until 38 [38: 42: 42: 46] sts rem in raglan armhole shaping.
Work 1 row, ending with RS facing for next row.

Shape front neck

Next row (RS): K3, sl 1, K1, psso, K4 [4: 6: 6: 8] and turn, leaving rem sts on a holder. 8 [8: 10: 10: 12] sts.
Work each side of neck separately.
Keeping raglan armhole decreases correct as set, dec 1 st at neck edge of next 3 [3: 3: 3: 4] rows **and at same time** dec 1 st at raglan armhole edge of 2nd and foll 0 [0: 0: 0: 1] alt row. 4 [4: 6: 6: 6] sts.

Sizes L, XL and XXL only

Work – [-: 0: 0: 1] row, ending with RS facing for next row.
Next row (RS): K3, sl 1, K2tog, psso. 4 sts.
Work 1 row.

All sizes

Next row (RS): K1, sl 1, K2tog, psso.
Next row: P2.
Next row: K2tog and fasten off.
With RS facing, slip centre 20 sts onto a holder, rejoin yarn, K to last 5 sts, K2tog, K3. 8 [8: 10: 10: 12] sts.
Complete to match first side, reversing shapings.

SLEEVES

Using 6mm (US 10) needles cast on 34 [36: 38: 38: 40] sts.
Row 1 (WS): K2 [3: 4: 4: 5], (P2, K2, P2, K6) twice, P2, K2, P2, K2 [3: 4: 4: 5].
Beg and ending rows as indicated and repeating the 24 row patt repeat throughout, cont in patt from chart as folls:
Inc 1 st at each end of 5th and every foll 6th row to 52 [52: 52: 60: 62] sts, then on every foll 8th row until there are 58 [60: 62: 64: 66] sts, taking inc sts into patt.
Cont straight until sleeve meas 44 [45: 46: 46: 46] cm, ending with RS facing for next row.

Shape raglan

Keeping patt correct, cast off 3 sts at beg of next 2 rows.
52 [54: 56: 58: 60] sts.
Dec 1 st at each end of next 11 rows, then on every foll alt row until 14 sts rem.
Work 1 row, ending with RS facing for next row.

Left sleeve only

Dec 1 st at each end of next row, then cast off 2 sts at beg of foll row. 10 sts.
Dec 1 st at beg of next row, then cast off 3 sts at beg of foll row. 6 sts.
Rep last 2 rows once more.

Right sleeve only

Cast off 3 sts at beg and dec 1 st at end of next row. 10 sts.
Work 1 row.
Rep last 2 rows twice more.

Both sleeves
Cast off rem 2 sts.

MAKING UP
Press as described on the information page.
Join both front and right back raglan seams using back stitch, or mattress stitch if preferred.

Neckband
With RS facing and using 6mm (US 10) needles, pick up and knit 8 sts from top of left sleeve, and 5 [5: 7: 7: 9] sts down left side of front neck, K across 20 sts on front holder, pick up and knit 5 [5: 7: 7: 9] sts up right side of front neck, and 8 sts from top of right sleeve, then K across 26 [26: 28: 28: 30] sts on back holder. 72 [72: 78: 78: 84] sts.
Work in g st for 2 rows, ending with **WS** facing for next row.
Cast off knitwise (on **WS**).
See information page for finishing instructions.

Front crochet trim (optional)
Using 2.50mm (US C2) crochet hook and Rowan Fine Tweed, make a length of ch that fits neatly along pick-up row of neckband between raglan seams, working a multiple of 8 ch plus 3 extra. (**Note**: As a foundation ch has a tendency to be a little tight, remember to work this ch quite loosely. And, as crochet has a tendency to shrink in width as it is worked, make the length of ch a little longer, rather than shorter, to achieve the correct number of ch.)

Row 1 (RS): 1 tr into 4th ch from hook, 1 tr into each ch to end, turn. (You should now have a multiple of 8 tr plus 3 ch at beg of row.)
Row 2: 1 ch (does NOT count as st), 1 dc into each of first 3 tr, *2 ch, miss 1 tr, (2 tr, 2 ch and 2 tr) into next tr, 2 ch, miss 1 tr**, 1 dc into each of next 5 tr, rep from * to end, ending last rep at **, 1 dc into each of last 3 sts, turn.
Row 3: 1 ch (does NOT count as st), 1 dc into each of first 2 dc, *3 ch, miss (1 dc, 2 ch and 2 tr), (3 tr, 2 ch and 3 tr) into next ch sp, 3 ch, miss (2 tr, 2 ch and 1 dc**, 1 dc into each of next 3 dc, rep from * to end, ending last rep at **, 1 dc into each of last 2 dc, turn.
Row 4: 1 ch (does NOT count as st), 1 dc into first dc, *4 ch, miss (1 dc, 3 ch and 3 tr), (4 tr, 2 ch and 4 tr) into next ch sp, 4 ch, miss (3 tr, 2 ch and 1 dc), 1 dc into next dc, rep from * to end, turn.
Row 5: 1 ch (does NOT count as st), 1 dc into first dc, *6 ch, miss (4 ch and 4 tr), (4 tr, 2 ch and 4 tr) into next ch sp, 6 ch, miss (4 tr and 4 ch), 1 dc into next dc, rep from * to end.
Fasten off.
Lay completed crochet trim against RS of front, with foundation ch edge against neckband pick-up row. Neatly sew in place along raglan armhole edges and neckband pick-up row.

Back crochet trim (optional)
Work as given for front crochet trim, attaching this trim to back neck edge.

LEAF WAISTCOAT ●●●

To fit bust	S	M	L	XL	XXL	
	81-86	91-97	102-107	112-117	122-127	cm
	32-34	36-38	40-42	44-46	48-50	in
Rowan Felted Tweed						
A Treacle 145	3	3	4	4	4	x 50gm
B Tawny 186	1	1	1	2	2	x 50gm
C Peony 183	1	1	1	1	1	x 50gm
D Hedgerow 187	1	1	1	1	1	x 50gm
E Ginger 154	1	1	1	1	1	x 50gm
F Cinnamon 175	1	1	1	1	1	x 50gm
G Rage 150	1	1	1	1	1	x 50gm

Needles
1 pair 2¾mm (no 12) (US 2) needles
1 pair 3¼mm (no 10) (US 3) needles
2¾mm (no 12) (US 2) circular needle

Buttons – 8 x 15mm antique gunmetal buttons – see information page for suggested suppliers.

Tension
29 sts and 30 rows to 10 cm measured over patterned st st using 3¼mm (US 3) needles.

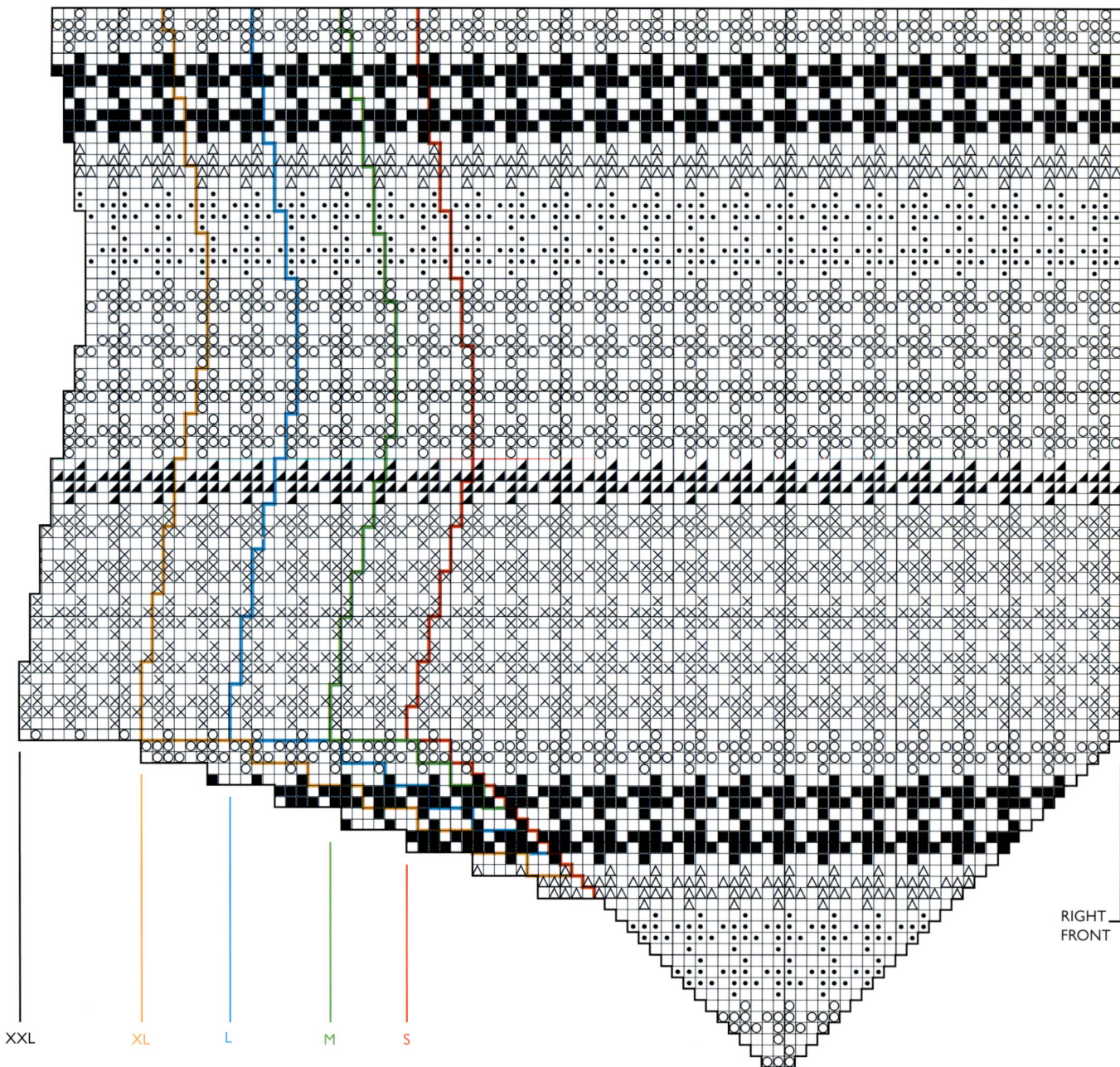

RIGHT
FRONT

XXL   XL   L   M   S

KEY

A □ Treacle 145   C ◢ Peony 183   E • Ginger 154   G ■ Rage 150

B ✕ Tawny 186   D ○ Hedgerow 187   F △ Cinnamon 175

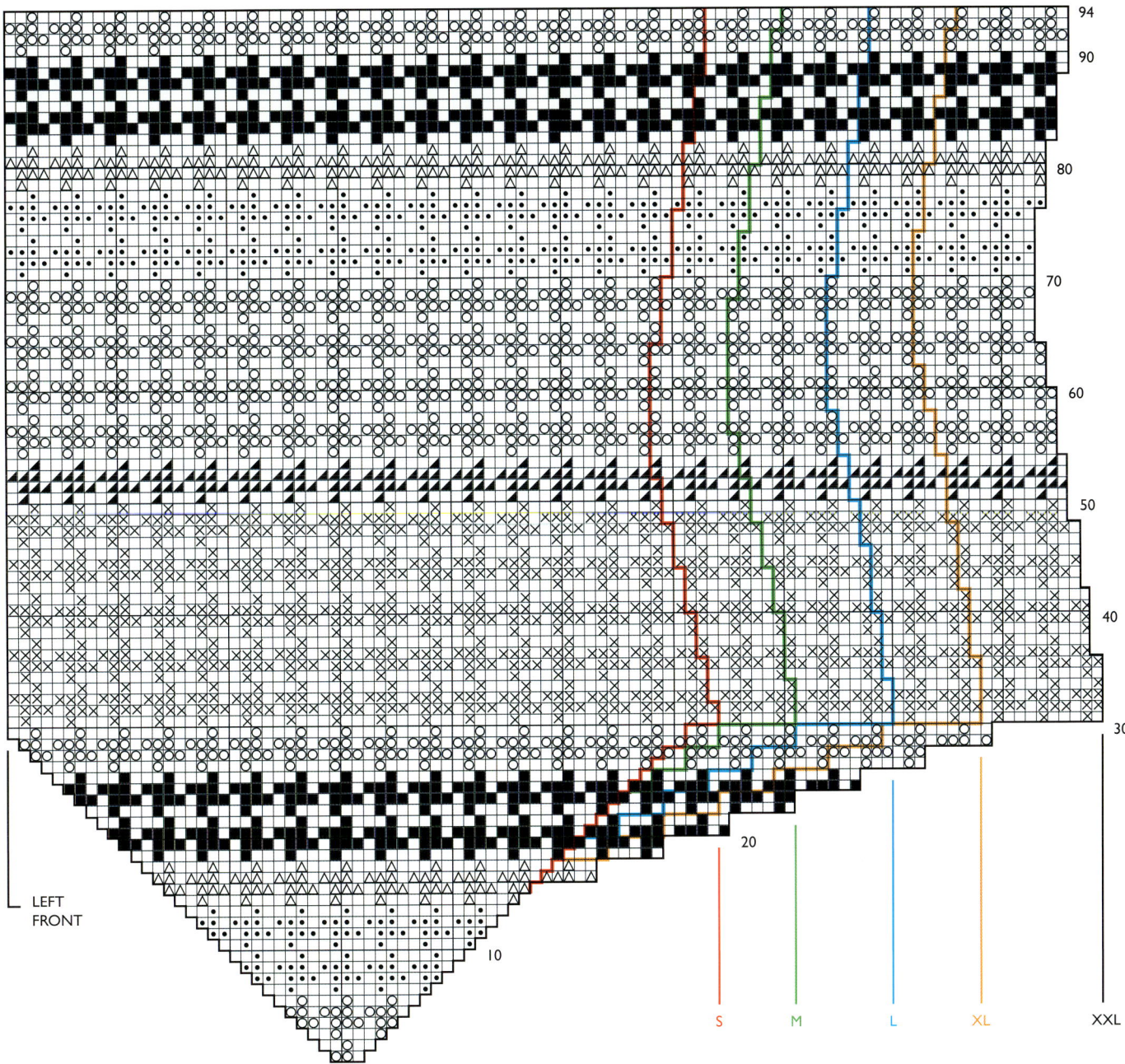

94

90

80

70

60

50

40

30

64 row pattern repeat

LEFT
FRONT

20

10

S   M   L   XL   XXL

49

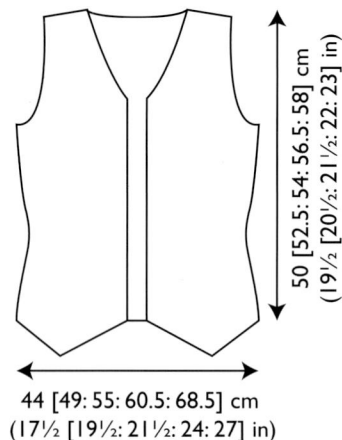

50 [52.5: 54: 56.5: 58] cm
(19½ [20½: 21½: 22: 23] in)

44 [49: 55: 60.5: 68.5] cm
(17½ [19½: 21½: 24: 27] in)

BACK

Using 3¼mm (US 3) needles and yarn A cast on 128 [142: 160: 176: 198] sts.
Beg and ending rows as indicated, using the **fairisle** technique as described on the information page and repeating the 64 row patt repeat throughout, cont in patt from chart, which is worked entirely in st st beg with a K row, as folls:
Beg with chart row **31**, dec 1 st at each end of 3rd [5th: 5th: 7th: 7th] and 0 [1: 2: 3: 4] foll 6th rows, then on 5 [4: 3: 2: 1] foll 4th rows.
116 [130: 148: 164: 186] sts.
Work 11 rows, ending with RS facing for next row.
Inc 1 st at each end of next and 5 foll 6th rows, taking inc sts into patt.
128 [142: 160: 176: 198] sts.
Work 15 rows, ending with RS facing for next row. (Back should meas 26.5 [28: 28.5: 30: 30.5] cm.)

Shape armholes

Keeping patt correct, cast off 5 [6: 8: 9: 11] sts at beg of next 2 rows.
118 [130: 144: 158: 176] sts.
Dec 1 st at each end of next 5 [7: 7: 9: 11] rows, then on foll 4 [5: 7: 8: 10] alt rows, then on foll 4th row. 98 [104: 114: 122: 132] sts.
Cont straight until armhole meas 20 [21: 22: 23: 24] cm, ending with RS facing for next row.

Shape shoulders and back neck

Next row (RS): Cast off 5 [6: 7: 8: 9] sts, patt until there are 21 [23: 26: 29: 32] sts on right needle and turn, leaving rem sts on a holder.
Work each side of neck separately.
Dec 1 st at neck edge of next 4 rows **and at same time** cast off 5 [6: 7: 8: 9] sts at beg of 2nd row, then 6 [6: 7: 8: 9] sts at beg of foll alt row.
Work 1 row.
Cast off rem 6 [7: 8: 9: 10] sts.
With RS facing, slip centre 46 [46: 48: 48: 50] sts onto a holder, rejoin yarns and patt to end.
Complete to match first side, reversing shapings.

LEFT FRONT

Using 3¼mm (US 3) needles and yarn A cast on 3 sts.
Beg and ending rows as indicated and beg with chart row **1**, cont in patt from chart as folls:

Work 1 row, ending with RS facing for next row.
Inc 1 st at each end of next 27 [23: 19: 17: 15] rows, taking inc sts into patt and ending with RS facing for next row. 57 [49: 41: 37: 33] sts.
Inc 1 st at end of next row and at same edge on foll 1 [5: 9: 11: 13] rows, ending with RS facing for next row, **and at same time** cast on 2 [3: 4: 5: 6] sts at beg of next and foll 0 [2: 4: 5: 6] alt rows. 61 [64: 71: 79: 89] sts.
Cast on 3 [7: 9: 9: 10] sts at beg of next row. 64 [71: 80: 88: 99] sts.
Place markers at both ends of last row.
This completes lower edge shaping.
Dec 1 st at beg of 2nd [4th: 4th: 6th: 6th] and 0 [1: 2: 3: 4] foll 6th rows, then on 5 [4: 3: 2: 1] foll 4th rows. 58 [65: 74: 82: 93] sts.
Work 11 rows, ending with RS facing for next row.
Inc 1 st at beg of next and 5 foll 6th rows, taking inc sts into patt.
64 [71: 80: 88: 99] sts.
Work 15 rows, ending with RS facing for next row.

Shape armhole

Keeping patt correct, cast off 5 [6: 8: 9: 11] sts at beg of next row.
59 [65: 72: 79: 88] sts.
Work 1 row.
Dec 1 st at armhole edge of next 5 [7: 7: 9: 10] rows, then on foll 2 [1: 1: 0: 0] alt rows. 52 [57: 64: 70: 78] sts.
Work 1 [1: 1: 1: 0] row, ending with RS facing for next row.

Shape front slope

Keeping patt correct, dec 1 st at end of next row and at same edge on foll 14 [10: 10: 6: 6] rows, then on foll 12 [16: 17: 21: 22] alt rows **and at same time** dec 1 st at armhole edge of next and foll 1 [3: 5: 7: 10] alt rows, then on foll 4th row. 22 [25: 29: 33: 37] sts.
Cont straight until left front matches back to beg of shoulder shaping, ending with RS facing for next row.

Shape shoulder

Cast off 5 [6: 7: 8: 9] sts at beg of next and foll alt row, then 6 [6: 7: 8: 9] sts at beg of foll alt row.
Work 1 row.
Cast off rem 6 [7: 8: 9: 10] sts.

RIGHT FRONT

Using 3¼mm (US 3) needles and yarn A cast on 3 sts.
Beg and ending rows as indicated and beg with chart row **1**, cont in patt from chart as folls:
Work 1 row, ending with RS facing for next row.
Inc 1 st at each end of next 26 [22: 18: 16: 14] rows, taking inc sts into patt and ending with **WS** facing for next row. 55 [47: 39: 35: 31] sts.
Inc 1 st at end of next row and at same edge on foll 1 [5: 9: 11: 13] rows, ending with **WS** facing for next row, **and at same time** cast on 2 [3: 4: 5: 6] sts at beg of next and foll 0 [2: 4: 5: 6] alt rows.
59 [62: 69: 77: 87] sts.
Cast on 4 [8: 10: 10: 11] sts at beg and inc 1 st at end of next row.
64 [71: 80: 88: 99] sts.
Work 1 row.
Place markers at both ends of last row.
This completes lower edge shaping.
Dec 1 st at end of 2nd [4th: 4th: 6th: 6th] and 0 [1: 2: 3: 4] foll 6th rows, then on 5 [4: 3: 2: 1] foll 4th rows. 58 [65: 74: 82: 93] sts.
Complete to match left front, reversing shapings.

MAKING UP

Press as described on the information page.

Join both shoulder seams using back stitch, or mattress stitch if preferred.

Back hem border

With RS facing, using 2¾mm (US 2) needles and yarn A, pick up and knit 123 [137: 155: 169: 191] sts evenly across back cast-on edge.

Row 1 (WS): K1, *P1, K1, rep from * to end.

Row 2: As row 1.

These 2 rows form moss st.

Work in moss st for 3 rows more, ending with RS facing for next row.

Cast off in moss st.

Front hem, opening edge and neck border

With RS facing, using 2¾mm (US 2) circular needle and yarn A, beg at marker at base of right side seam edge, pick up and knit 33 [40: 49: 57: 68] sts along shaped cast-on and inc row-end edge to centre of original 3 cast-on sts, 1 st from centre of this cast-on edge and mark this st with a coloured thread, 32 sts up next shaped row-end edge to marker at base of front opening edge, 1 st at marked point and mark this st with a coloured thread, 90 [92: 95: 98: 101] sts up right front opening edge to beg of front slope shaping, 48 [52: 54: 58: 60] sts up right front slope, and 7 sts down right side of back neck, K across 46 [46: 48: 48: 50] sts on back holder dec 1 st at centre, pick up and knit 7 sts up left side of back neck, 48 [52: 54: 58: 60] sts down left front slope to beg of front slope shaping, 90 [92: 95: 98: 101] sts down left front opening edge to marker at base of front opening edge, 1 st at marked point and mark this st with a coloured thread, 32 sts down next shaped row-end edge to

centre of original 3 cast-on sts, 1 st from centre of this cast-on edge and mark this st with a coloured thread, and 33 [40: 49: 57: 68] sts along shaped inc row-end and cast-on edge to marker at base of left side seam edge. 469 [495: 525: 555: 589] sts, 4 marked sts in total.

Work in moss st as given for back hem border for 1 row.

Row 2 (RS): (Moss st to marked st, inc **twice** in marked st and re-position marker on centre st of these 3 sts) 4 times, moss st to end. 477 [503: 533: 563: 597] sts.

Work 1 row.

Row 4: (Moss st to marked st, inc **twice** in marked st and re-position marker on centre st of these 3 sts) twice, moss st 2 [3: 2: 1: 3] sts, *yrn, work 2 tog (to make a buttonhole), moss st 15 [15: 16: 17: 17] sts, rep from * 4 times more, yrn, work 2 tog (to make 6th buttonhole), (moss st to marked st, inc **twice** in marked st and re-position marker on centre st of these 3 sts) twice, moss st to end. 485 [511: 541: 571: 605] sts.

Work 1 row, ending with RS facing for next row.

Cast off in moss st.

Armhole borders (both alike)

With RS facing, using 2¾mm (US 2) needles and yarn A, pick up and knit 121 [129: 139: 147: 157] sts evenly all round armhole edge.

Work in moss st as given for back hem border for 5 rows, ending with RS facing for next row.

Cast off in moss st.

See information page for finishing instructions. Using photograph as a guide, attach 2 buttons to lower left front hem border section.

PARSLEY ●●●

To fit bust	S	M	L	XL	XXL	
	81-86	91-97	102-107	112-117	122-127	cm
	32-34	36-38	40-42	44-46	48-50	in
Rowan Fine Tweed						
A Askrigg 365	5	5	6	7	7	x 25gm
B Settle 374	3	4	4	5	5	x 25gm
C Hubberholme 370	4	5	5	6	6	x 25gm
D Tissington 386	2	2	2	2	3	x 25gm
E Skipton 379	1	1	1	1	1	x 25gm
F Beresford 387	1	1	1	1	1	x 25gm
G Leyburn 383	1	1	1	2	2	x 25gm
H *Dent 373	1	1	1	1	1	x 25gm

*Yarn H is used for optional crochet trim only

Needles

1 pair 2¾mm (no 12) (US 2) needles
1 pair 3¼mm (no 10) (US 3) needles
2.50mm (no 12) (US C2) crochet hook (optional)

Buttons – 11 x 10mm metal ball buttons – see information page for suggested suppliers.

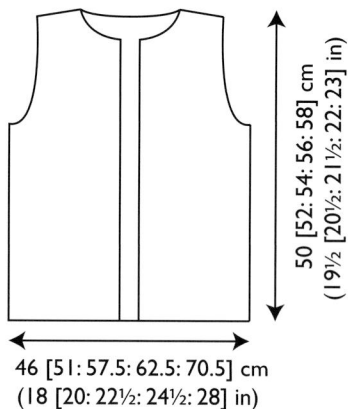

50 [52: 54: 56: 58] cm
(19½ [20½: 21½: 22: 23] in)

46 [51: 57.5: 62.5: 70.5] cm
(18 [20: 22½: 24½: 28] in)

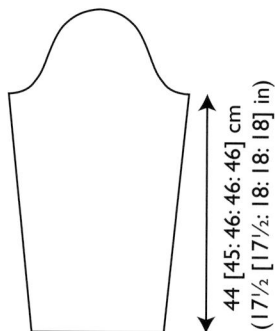

44 [45: 46: 46: 46] cm
(17½ [17½: 18: 18: 18] in)

Tension
26 sts and 32 rows to 10 cm measured over patterned st st using 3¼mm (US 3) needles.

Crochet abbreviations
ch = chain; **dc** = double crochet; **sp(s)** = space(s); **tr** = treble.
See information page for US abbreviations.

BACK
Using 2¾mm (US 2) needles and yarn A cast on 119 [133: 149: 163: 183] sts.
Break off yarn A and join in yarn C.
Row 1 (WS): K1, *P1, K1, rep from * to end.
Row 2: As row 1.
These 2 rows form moss st.
Work in moss st for a further 5 rows, ending with RS facing for next row.
Change to 3¼mm (US 3) needles.
Beg and ending rows as indicated, using the **fairisle** technique as described on the information page and repeating the 42 row patt repeat throughout, cont in patt from chart, which is worked entirely in st st beg with a K row, as folls:

KEY

A. ☐ Askrigg 365
C. ○ Hubberholme 370
E. ∧ Skipton 379

B. ✕ Settle 374
D. ▲ Tissington 386
F. \ Beresford 387
G. • Leyburn 383

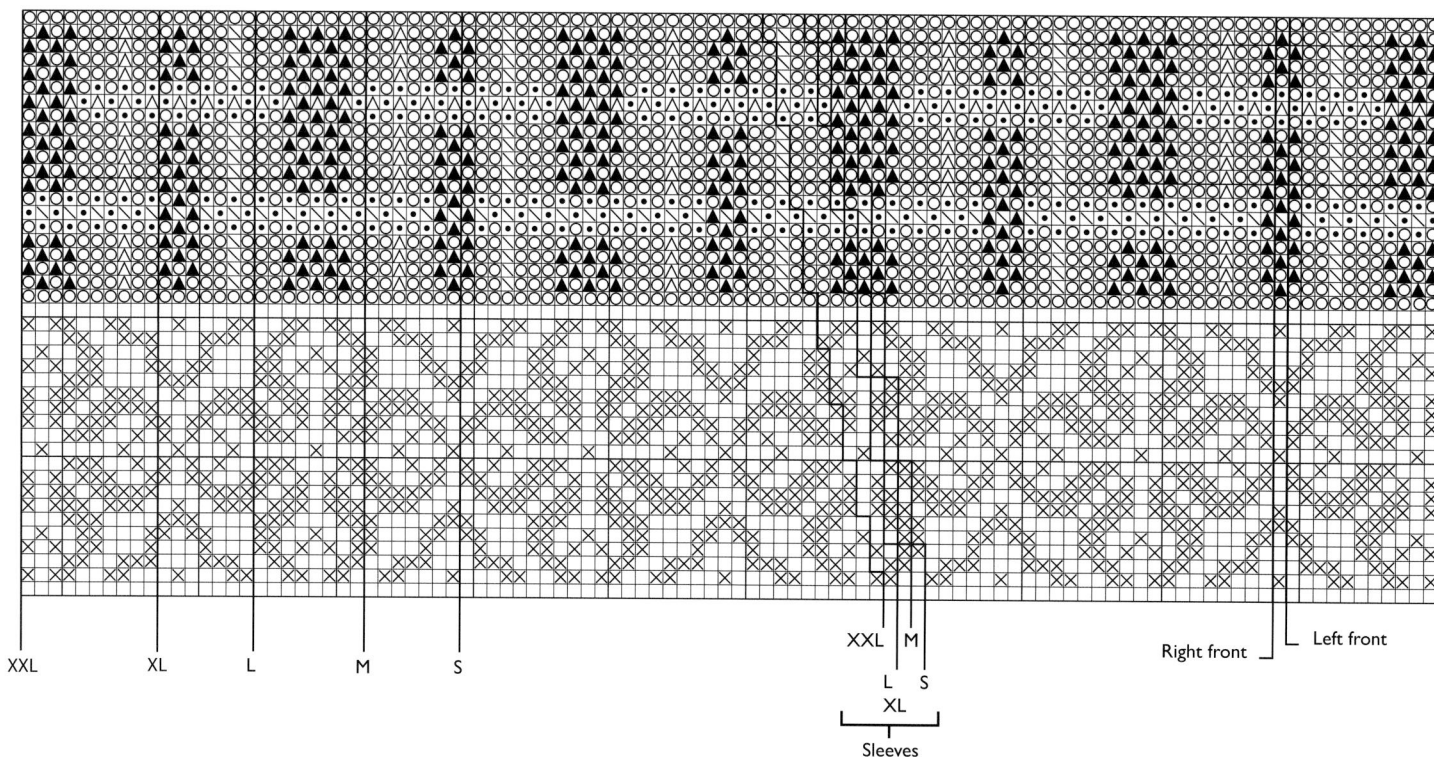

Cont straight until back meas 30 [31: 32: 33: 34] cm, ending with RS facing for next row.

Shape armholes

Keeping patt correct, cast off 5 [7: 8: 9: 11] sts at beg of next 2 rows. 109 [119: 133: 145: 161] sts.

Dec 1 st at each end of next 5 [7: 9: 9: 11] rows, then on foll 5 [6: 7: 9: 10] alt rows. 89 [93: 101: 109: 119] sts.

Cont straight until armhole meas 18 [19: 20: 21: 22] cm, ending with RS facing for next row.

Shape shoulders and back neck

Next row (RS): Cast off 5 [5: 6: 7: 8] sts, patt until there are 20 [22: 24: 27: 30] sts on right needle and turn, leaving rem sts on a holder.

Work each side of neck separately.

Dec 1 st at neck edge of next 4 rows **and at same time** cast off 5 [6: 6: 7: 8] sts at beg of 2nd row, then 5 [6: 7: 8: 9] sts at beg of foll alt row.

Work 1 row.

Cast off rem 6 [6: 7: 8: 9] sts.

With RS facing, slip centre 39 [39: 41: 41: 43] sts onto a holder, rejoin yarns and patt to end.

Complete to match first side, reversing shapings.

LEFT FRONT

Using 2¾mm (US 2) needles and yarn A cast on 59 [65: 73: 81: 91] sts.

Break off yarn A and join in yarn C.

Work in moss st as given for back for 7 rows, inc 0 [1: 1: 0: 0] st at end of last row and ending with RS facing for next row. 59 [66: 74: 81: 91] sts.

Change to 3¼mm (US 3) needles.

Beg and ending rows as indicated, cont in patt from chart as folls:

Cont straight until left front matches back to beg of armhole shaping, ending with RS facing for next row.

Shape armhole

Keeping patt correct, cast off 5 [7: 8: 9: 11] sts at beg of next row. 54 [59: 66: 72: 80] sts.

Work 1 row.

Dec 1 st at armhole edge of next 5 [7: 9: 9: 11] rows, then on foll 5 [6: 7: 9: 10] alt rows. 44 [46: 50: 54: 59] sts.

Cont straight until 20 [20: 22: 22: 24] rows less have been worked than on back to beg of shoulder shaping, ending with RS facing for next row.

Shape front neck

Next row (RS): Patt 33 [35: 39: 43: 48] sts and turn, leaving rem 11 sts on a holder (for neckband).

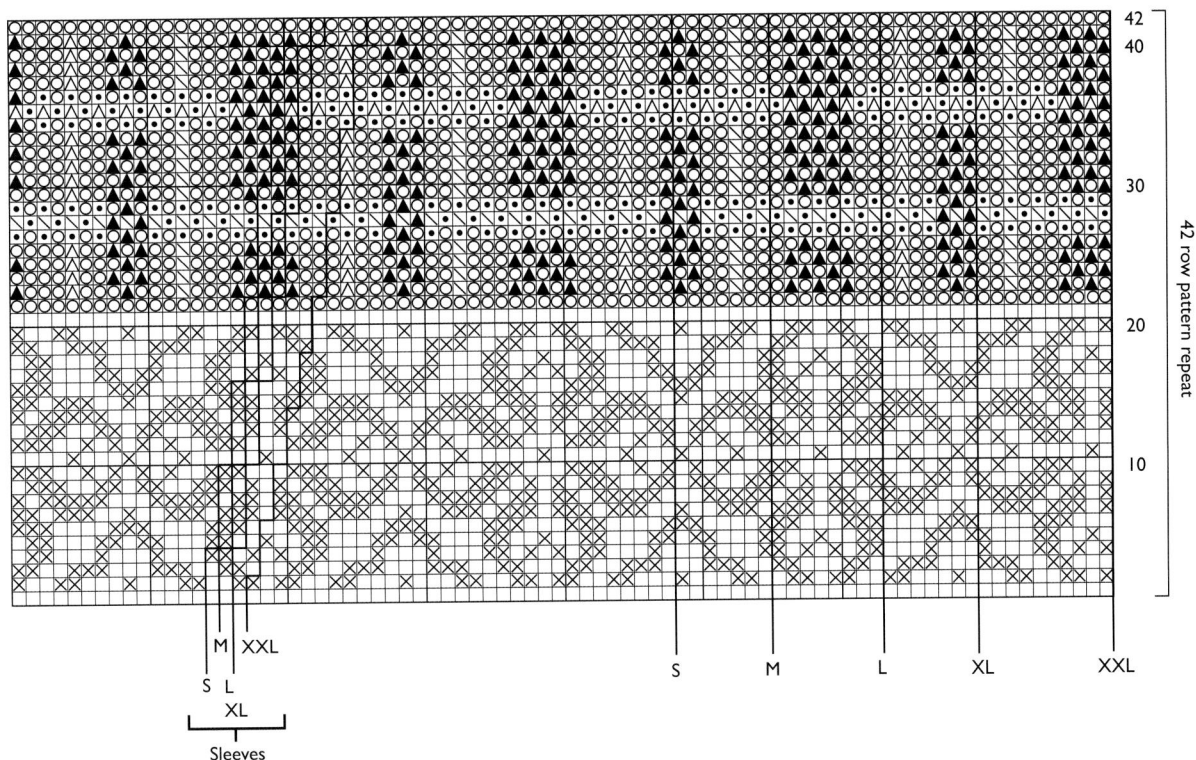

Keeping patt correct, dec 1 st at neck edge of next 8 rows, then on foll 3 [3: 4: 4: 5] alt rows, then on foll 4th row. 21 [23: 26: 30: 34] sts.
Work 1 row, ending with RS facing for next row.

Shape shoulder

Cast off 5 [5: 6: 7: 8] sts at beg of next and 2 [0: 1: 1: 1] alt rows, then 0 [6: 7: 8: 9] sts at beg of foll 0 [2: 1: 1: 1] alt rows.
Work 1 row.
Cast off rem 6 [6: 7: 8: 9] sts.

RIGHT FRONT

Work to match left front, reversing shapings and working first row of front neck shaping as folls:

Shape front neck

Next row (RS): Break yarns and slip first 11 sts onto a holder (for neckband). Rejoin yarns and patt to end. 33 [35: 39: 43: 48] sts.

SLEEVES

Using 2¾mm (US 2) needles and yarn A cast on 51 [53: 55: 55: 57] sts.
Break off yarn A and join in yarn C.
Work in moss st as given for back for 7 rows, ending with RS facing for next row.
Change to 3¼mm (US 3) needles.
Beg and ending rows as indicated, cont in patt from chart as folls:
Inc 1 st at each end of 5th [5th: 5th: 5th: 3rd] and every foll 6th [6th: 6th: 6th: 4th] row to 59 [73: 81: 97: 69] sts, then on every foll 8th [8th: 8th: -: 6th] row until there are 83 [89: 93: -: 103] sts, taking inc sts into patt.
Cont straight until sleeve meas 44 [45: 46: 46: 46] cm, ending with RS facing for next row.

Shape top

Keeping patt correct, cast off 5 [7: 8: 9: 11] sts at beg of next 2 rows. 73 [75: 77: 79: 81] sts.
Dec 1 st at each end of next 5 rows, then on foll 3 alt rows, then on 2 foll 4th rows. 53 [55: 57: 59: 61] sts.
Work 1 row.
Dec 1 st at each end of next and every foll alt row until 41 sts rem, then on foll 9 rows, ending with RS facing for next row. 23 sts.
Cast off 4 sts at beg of next 2 rows.
Cast off rem 15 sts.

MAKING UP

Press as described on the information page.
Join both shoulder seams using back stitch, or mattress stitch if preferred.

Button band

With RS facing, using 2¾mm (US 2) needles and yarn C, pick up and knit 113 [123: 123: 123: 133] sts evenly down left front opening edge, from neck shaping to cast-on edge.
Work in moss st as given for back for 3 rows, ending with RS facing for next row.
Break off yarn C and join in yarn A.
Cast off in moss st.

Buttonhole band

With RS facing, using 2¾mm (US 2) needles and yarn C, pick up and knit 113 [123: 123: 123: 133] sts evenly up right front opening edge, from cast-on edge to neck shaping.
Work in moss st as given for back for 1 row, ending with RS facing for next row.
Row 2 (RS): Moss st 3 sts, *work 2 tog, yrn (to make a buttonhole), moss st 9 [10: 10: 10: 11] sts, rep from * to end.
Work in moss st for a further 1 row, ending with RS facing for next row.
Break off yarn C and join in yarn A.
Cast off in moss st.

Neckband

With RS facing, using 2¾mm (US 2) needles and yarn C, beg and ending at cast-off edges of front bands, pick up and knit 3 sts from row-end edge of buttonhole band, K across 11 sts on right front holder, pick up and knit 20 [20: 22: 22: 24] sts up right side of front neck, and 5 sts down right side of back neck, K across 39 [39: 41: 41: 43] sts on back holder, pick up and knit 5 sts up left side of back neck, and 20 [20: 22: 22: 24] sts down left side of front neck, K across 11 sts on left front holder, then pick up and knit 3 sts from row-end edge of button band.
117 [117: 123: 123: 129] sts.
Work in moss st as given for back for 1 row, ending with RS facing for next row.
Row 2 (RS): Moss st 1 st, work 2 tog, yrn (to make 11th buttonhole), moss st to end.
Work in moss st for a further 1 row, ending with RS facing for next row.
Break off yarn C and join in yarn A.
Cast off in moss st.
See information page for finishing instructions, setting in sleeves using the set-in method.

Crochet trim (make 2 – optional)

Using 2.50mm (US C2) crochet hook and yarn H, make a length of ch that fits neatly along front opening edge, from neck shaping to start of fairisle pattern and working a multiple of 12 ch. (**Note:** As a foundation ch has a tendency to be a little tight, remember to work this ch quite loosely. And, as crochet has a tendency to shrink in width as it is worked, make the length of ch a little longer, rather than shorter, to achieve the correct number of ch.)
Row 1 (RS): 1 dc into 2nd ch from hook, *(5 ch, miss 4 ch, 1 dc into next ch) twice**, (5 ch, 1 dc into next ch) twice, rep from * to end, ending last rep at **, turn.
Row 2: 6 ch (counts as 1 tr and 3 ch), miss dc at base of 6 ch, 1 dc into first ch sp, *3 ch, miss 1 dc, 1 dc into next ch sp, rep from * until dc has been worked in last ch sp, 3 ch, 1 tr into last dc, turn.
Row 3: 1 ch (does NOT count as st), 1 dc into tr at base of 1 ch, 5 ch, miss 1 dc, *(1 dc, 5 ch, 1 dc, 5 ch and 1 dc) into next ch sp, 5 ch**, miss (1 dc, 3 ch and 1 dc), 1 dc into next ch sp, 5 ch, miss (1 dc, 3 ch and 1 dc), rep from * to end, ending last rep at **, miss 1 dc, 1 dc into 3rd of 6 ch at beg of previous row.
Fasten off.

Using the photograph as a guide, with RS of optional crochet trim and each front facing, place one crochet trim against the button band and the other against the buttonhole band and stitch neatly in place.

ROSEMARY ●●

	S	M	L	XL	XXL	
To fit bust	81-86	91-97	102-107	112-117	122-127	cm
	32-34	36-38	40-42	44-46	48-50	in

Rowan Felted Tweed

		S	M	L	XL	XXL	
A	Watery 152	6	7	8	9	10	× 50gm
B	Avocado 161	1	1	1	1	1	× 50gm
C	Paisley 171	1	1	1	1	1	× 50gm
D	Gilt 160	1	1	1	1	1	× 50gm
E	Ginger 154	1	1	1	1	1	× 50gm
F	Cinnamon 175	1	1	1	1	1	× 50gm
G	Hedgerow 187	1	1	1	1	1	× 50gm
H	Peony 183	1	1	1	1	1	× 50gm
I	Bilberry 151	2	2	2	2	2	× 50gm

Needles

1 pair 2¾mm (no 12) (US 2) needles
1 pair 3¼mm (no 10) (US 3) needles
3.00mm (no 11) (US C2) crochet hook

Buttons – 7 × 18mm antique gunmetal buttons – see information page for suggested suppliers.

Tension

24 sts and 38 rows to 10 cm measured over moss st using 3¼mm (US 3) needles. Each motif is 9 cm square.

Crochet abbreviations

ch = chain; **dc** = double crochet; **dtr** = double treble; **sp(s)** = space(s); **ss** = slip stitch; **tr** = treble; **tr2tog** = (yoh and insert hook as indicated, yoh and draw loop through, yoh and draw through 2 loops) twice, yoh and draw through all 3 loops on hook; **yoh** = yarn over hook.
See information page for US abbreviations.

BACK
Main section
Using 3¼mm (US 3) needles and yarn A cast on 111 [123: 137: 151: 169] sts.
Row 1 (RS): K1, *P1, K1, rep from * to end.
Row 2: As row 1.
These 2 rows form moss st.
Cont in moss st until back meas 43 [45: 47: 49: 51] cm, ending with RS facing for next row.
Shape shoulders and back neck
Next row (RS): Cast off 6 [8: 9: 10: 12] sts, moss st until there are 34 [38: 43: 49: 55] sts on right needle and turn, leaving rem sts on a holder.
Work each side of neck separately.
Dec 1 st at neck edge of next 6 rows **and at same time** cast off 7 [8: 9: 10: 12] sts at beg of 2nd and foll 2 [2: 2: 0: 2] alt rows, then – [-: -: 11: -] sts at beg of foll – [-: 2: -] alt rows.
Work 1 row.
Cast off rem 7 [8: 10: 11: 13] sts.
With RS facing, rejoin yarn and cast off centre 31 [31: 33: 33: 35] sts, moss st to end.
Complete to match first side, reversing shapings.
Lower border
With RS facing, using 2¾mm (US 2) needles and yarn A, pick up and knit 110 [122: 138: 150: 170] sts evenly along cast-on edge of main section.
Row 1 (WS): P2, *K2, P2, rep from * to end.
Row 2: K2, *P2, K2, rep from * to end.
These 2 rows form rib.
Work in rib until lower border meas 7 cm from pick-up row, ending with RS facing for next row.
Cast off in rib.

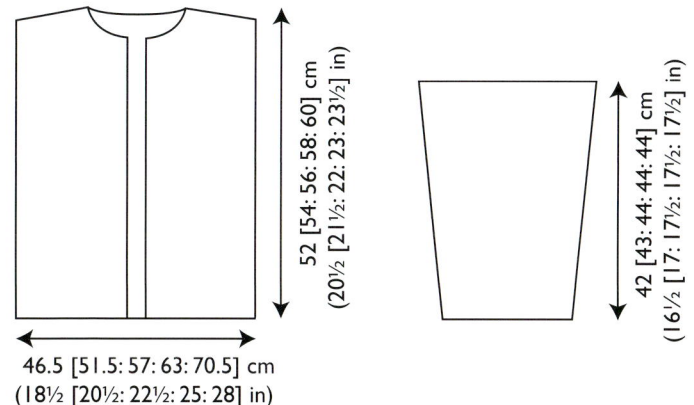

52 [54: 56: 58: 60] cm
(20½ [21½: 22: 23: 23½] in)

46.5 [51.5: 57: 63: 70.5] cm
(18½ [20½: 22½: 25: 28] in)

42 [43: 44: 44: 44] cm
(16½ [17: 17½: 17½: 17½] in)

FRONT MOTIF PANELS (make 2)
Motif A (make 6 [6: 6: 9: 9])
Using 3.00mm (US C2) crochet hook and yarn B, make 10 ch and join with a ss to form a ring.

Round 1: 3 ch (counts as 1 tr), 31 tr into ring, ss to top of 3 ch at beg of round.

Joining in and breaking off colours as required, cont as folls:

Round 2: Using yarn C, 1 ss into same place as ss at end of previous round, (7 ch, miss 3 tr, 1 ss into next tr) 7 times, 3 ch, miss 3 tr, 1 dtr into ss at beg of round.

Round 3: Using yarn A, 3 ch (counts as 1 tr), 6 tr into st at base of 3 ch, *miss (3 ch, 1 ss and 3 ch)**, 7 tr into next ch, rep from * to end, ending last rep at **, ss to top of 3 ch at beg of round.

Round 4: Using yarn D, ss across and into next tr (this is 2nd st of this first 7 st group), 6 ch (counts as 1 tr and 3 ch), *miss 1 tr, (1 dtr, 5 ch and 1 dtr) into next tr, 3 ch, miss 1 tr, tr2tog over next 4 tr working first "leg" into next tr, missing 2 tr and working second "leg" into next tr, 3 ch, miss 1 tr, 1 dc into next tr, 3 ch, miss 1 tr**, tr2tog over next 4 tr working first "leg" into next tr, missing 2 tr and working second "leg" into next tr, 3 ch, rep from * to end, ending last rep at **, 1 tr into next tr, 1 ss into 3rd of 6 ch at beg of round.

Round 5: Using yarn E, 1 ch (does NOT count as st), 1 dc into st at base of 1 ch, *3 dc into next ch sp, 1 dc into next dtr, 6 dc into next (corner) ch sp - place marker after 3rd of these 6 dc to mark actual corner point, 1 dc into next dtr, (3 dc into next ch sp, 1 dc into next st) 3 times, rep from * to end, replacing dc at end of last rep with ss to first dc. Fasten off.

Completed motif A is a square and along each side of square there are 23 dc between marked corner points.

Motif B (make 6 [6: 6: 9: 9])
Using 3.00mm (US C2) crochet hook and yarn E, make 6 ch and join with a ss to form a ring.

Round 1: 3 ch (counts as 1 tr), 15 tr into ring, ss to top of 3 ch at beg of round.

Joining in and breaking off colours as required, cont as folls:

Round 2: Using yarn F, 3 ch (counts as 1 tr), 2 tr into st at base of 3 ch, *2 ch, miss 1 tr, 1 tr into next tr, 2 ch, miss 1 tr**, 3 tr into next tr, rep from * to end, ending last rep at **, ss to top of 3 ch at beg of round.

Round 3: Using yarn G, 3 ch (counts as 1 tr), miss st at base of 3 ch, *5 tr into next tr, (1 tr into next tr, 2 ch, miss 2 ch) twice**, 1 tr into next tr, rep from * to end, ending last rep at **, ss to top of 3 ch at beg of round.

Round 4: Using yarn H, 3 ch (counts as 1 tr), miss st at base of 3 ch, 1 tr into each of next 2 tr, *5 tr into next tr, 1 tr into each of next 3 tr, 2 ch, miss 2 ch, 1 tr into next tr, 2 ch, miss 2 ch**, 1 tr into each of next 3 tr, rep from * to end, ending last rep at **, ss to top of 3 ch at beg of previous round.

Round 5: Using yarn B, 3 ch (counts as 1 tr), miss st at base of 3 ch, 1 tr into each of next 4 tr, *5 tr into next tr - place marker on 3rd of these 5 tr to mark actual corner point, 1 tr into each of next 5 tr, 2 tr into next ch sp, 1 tr into next tr, 2 tr into next ch sp**, 1 tr into each of next 5 tr, rep from * to end, ending last rep at **, ss to top of 3 ch at beg of round. Fasten off.

Completed motif B is a square. In each corner of square there is a (marked) tr, and there are a further 19 tr along each side between these marked sts.

Join motifs
Each motif is joined to the next motif with a row of tr worked using yarn I. Join motifs to form vertical bands of motifs, then join these strips of motifs to form a rectangle. Positions for motifs are shown on relevant motif layout diagrams, and motifs form a checkerboard effect. Each motif panel is 2 [2: 2: 3: 3] motifs wide, and 3 motifs deep.

To join one motif to adjacent motif, start by attaching yarn I by working a ss into a dc next to marked corner point of motif A, 1 tr into marked corner tr of adjacent motif B, (1 ss into next dc along side of motif A, 1 tr into next tr along side of motif B) 10 times, miss 1 dc along side of motif A, (1 ss into next dc along side of motif A, 1 tr into next tr along side of motif B) 10 times – tr at end of last rep is worked into corner tr at other end of this edge of motif B, 1 ss into next dc along side of motif A – this is dc next to other marked corner point of motif A. Fasten off.

Cont joining motifs to form 4 [4: 4: 6: 6] strips of 3 motifs.

Now work a row of tr along ends of each strip and fasten off. (Each strip should now meas approx 31 cm long.)

Now join strips to form shapes shown in layout diagrams in a similar way, work 3 sts into each row-end edge of the tr rows joining motifs, and fasten off.

Now work a row of tr along front opening edge of joined motifs and fasten off.

Now work a row of tr along side seam edge of joined motifs but do **NOT** fasten off, turn.

Next row: 3 ch (counts as 1 tr), miss tr at base of 3 ch, 1 tr into each st to end, turn.

Working last st of every foll row into top of 3 ch at beg of previous row (so number of sts remains the same), rep last row until work meas 23 [25.5: 28.5: 31.5: 35] cm from front opening edge.

Note: It is important to get this measurement correct as it affects the final width of the garment. It is better to work one extra row (so measurement is slightly greater than stated) than not to work enough rows. Fasten off.

LEFT FRONT
Yoke
With RS facing, using 3¼mm (US 3) needles and yarn A, pick up and knit 55 [61: 68: 75: 84] sts evenly across top of left front motif panel.

Row 1 (WS): K1 [1: 0: 1: 0], *P1, K1, rep from * to end.

Row 2: *K1, P1, rep from * to last 1 [1: 0: 1: 0] st, K1 [1: 0: 1: 0].

These 2 rows form moss st.

Work in moss st until left front meas 37 [39: 40: 42: 43] cm from lower edge of motif panel, ending with **WS** facing for next row.

Shape front neck
Cast off 8 sts at beg of next row. 47 [53: 60: 67: 76] sts.

Dec 1 st at neck edge of next 9 rows, then on foll 3 alt rows, then on 1 [1: 2: 2: 3] foll 4th rows. 34 [40: 46: 53: 61] sts.

Work 3 rows, ending with RS facing for next row. (Left front should meas 43 [45: 47: 49: 51] cm from lower edge of motif panel.)

Shape shoulder
Cast off 6 [8: 9: 10: 12] sts at beg of next and foll 0 [3: 3: 1: 3] alt rows, then 7 [-: -: 11: -] sts at beg of foll 3 [-: -: 2: -] alt rows.

Work 1 row.

FRONT MOTIF PANELS

SIZES S, M, & L

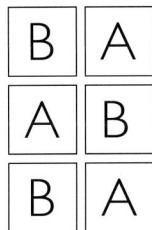 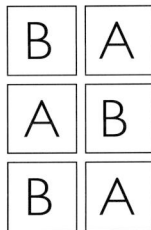

Right front   Left front

SIZES XL & XXL

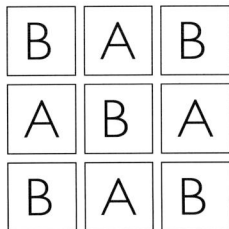 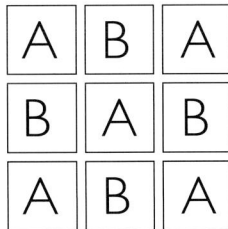

Right front   Left front

SLEEVE MOTIF PANELS

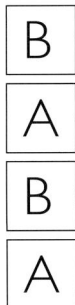

Cast off rem 7 [8: 10: 11: 13] sts.

Lower border

With RS facing, using 2¾mm (US 2) needles and yarn A, pick up and knit 55 [63: 67: 75: 83] sts evenly across lower edge of left front motif panel.

Row 1 (WS): P2, *K2, P2, rep from * to last st, K1.

Row 2: K3, *P2, K2, rep from * to end.

These 2 rows form rib.

Work in rib until lower border meas 7 cm from pick-up row, ending with RS facing for next row.

Cast off in rib.

RIGHT FRONT

Yoke

With RS facing, using 3¼mm (US 3) needles and yarn A, pick up and knit 55 [61: 68: 75: 84] sts evenly across top of right front motif panel.

Row 1 (WS): *K1, P1, rep from * to last 1 [1: 0: 1: 0] st, K1 [1: 0: 1: 0].

Row 2: K1 [1: 0: 1: 0], *P1, K1, rep from * to end.

These 2 rows form moss st.

Complete to match yoke of left front, reversing shapings.

Lower border

With RS facing, using 2¾mm (US 2) needles and yarn A, pick up and knit 55 [63: 67: 75: 83] sts evenly across lower edge of right front motif panel.

Row 1 (WS): K1, P2, *K2, P2, rep from * to end.

Row 2: K2, *P2, K2, rep from * to last st, K1.

These 2 rows form rib.

Work in rib until lower border meas 7 cm from pick-up row, ending with RS facing for next row.

Cast off in rib.

SLEEVES

Underarm section

Using 3¼mm (US 3) needles and yarn A cast on 23 [25: 27: 27: 29] sts.

Work in moss st as given for back for 6 [4: 4: 4: 2] rows, ending with RS facing for next row.

Place marker on centre st of last row – this marks "sleeve seam" point of sleeve.

Next row (RS): Moss st to marked st, inc **twice** in marked st and re-position marker on centre st of these 3 sts, moss st to end.

Working all increases as set by last row, inc 2 sts at marked centre st of 8th [6th: 6th: 6th: 6th] and every foll 8th [6th: 6th: 6th: 6th] row to 47 [33: 43: 59: 75] sts, then on every foll 10th [8th: 8th: 8th: -] row until there are 55 [61: 65: 69: -] sts, taking inc sts into moss st.

Cont straight until sleeve meas 41 cm, ending with RS facing for next row.

Cast off in moss st, leaving marker on centre st.

Motif panel

Make 2 of motif A and 2 of motif B as given for front motif panels.

Following sleeve motif layout diagram, join these motifs as given for front motif panels to form one strip of 4 motifs, with a row of tr worked across both ends – joined motif strip should meas 41 cm long.

Using yarn I, now join motif strip to row-end edges of underarm section by working a joining row of tr in same way as front motif panel strips are joined, working the ss of this joining row into row-end edges of knitted underarm panel.

Cuff edging

With RS facing, using 3.00mm (US C2) crochet hook and yarn I, attach

yarn at centre of cast-on edge of underarm section, 3 ch (counts as 1 tr), work 1 round of tr evenly around entire cuff edge of sleeve, ss to top of 3 ch at beg of round, turn.
Next round: 3 ch (counts as 1 tr), miss st at base of 3 ch, 1 tr into each tr to end, ss to top of 3 ch at beg of round, turn.
Rep last round 0 [1: 2: 2: 2] times more.
Fasten off.

MAKING UP
Press as described on the information page.
Join both shoulder seams using back stitch, or mattress stitch if preferred.
Button band
With RS facing, using 2¾mm (US 2) needles and yarn A, pick up and knit 116 [120: 124: 128: 132] sts evenly down entire left front opening edge, from neck shaping to cast-off edge of lower border.
Row 1 (WS): K1, P2, *K2, P2, rep from * to last st, K1.
Row 2: K3, *P2, K2, rep from * to last st, K1.
These 2 rows form rib.
Cont in rib for a further 11 rows, ending with RS facing for next row.
Cast off in rib.

Buttonhole band
Work to match button band, picking up sts along right front opening edge and making 7 buttonholes in row 6 as folls:
Row 6 (RS): Rib 4 [6: 6: 4: 6], *yrn, work 2 tog (to make a buttonhole), rib 16 [16: 17: 18: 18], rep from * 5 times more, yrn, work 2 tog (to make 7th buttonhole), rib 2 [4: 2: 2: 4].
Collar
Using 2¾mm (US 2) needles and yarn A cast on 140 [140: 148: 148: 156] sts.
Beg with row 2, work in rib as given for button band until collar meas 7 cm, ending with RS facing for next row.
Cast off 3 [3: 3: 3: 4] sts at beg of next 8 [8: 2: 2: 20] rows, then 4 [4: 4: 4: 5] sts at beg of foll 16 [16: 22: 22: 4] rows.
Cast off rem 52 [52: 54: 54: 56] sts.
Sew shaped cast-off edge of collar to neck edge, positioning row-end edges of collar midway across top of front borders.
Mark points along side seam edges 18 [19: 20: 21: 22] cm either side of shoulder seams, and then join side seams below these points. Now sew sleeves into armholes, matching marker on cast-off edge of sleeve to top of side seam and centre of motif strip to shoulder seam.
See information page for finishing instructions.

THYME WRAP ●●

One size only

Rowan Cocoon
11 x 100gm
(Photographed in Clay 825)
Needles
1 pair 6mm (no 4) (US 10) needles

Tension
24 sts and 22 rows to 10 cm measured over cable pattern using 6mm (US 10) needles.

Special abbreviations
C3B = slip next st onto cable needle and leave at back of work, K2, then K1 from cable needle. **C3F** = slip next 2 sts onto cable needle and leave at front of work, K1, then K2 from cable needle. **C4B** = slip next 2 sts onto cable needle and leave at back of work, K2, then K2 from cable needle. **C4F** = slip next 2 sts onto cable needle and leave at front of work, K2, then K2 from cable needle. **C5B** = slip next 3 sts onto cable needle and leave at back of work, K2, then K3 from cable needle. **C5F** = slip next 2 sts onto cable needle and leave at front of work, K3, then K2 from cable needle. **C6B** = slip next 3 sts onto cable needle and leave at back of work, K3, then K3 from cable needle. **C6F** = slip next 3 sts onto

cable needle and leave at front of work, K3, then K3 from cable needle.

Finished size
Completed wrap measures 58cm (23 ins) wide and 160cm (63 ins) long.

WRAP
Using 6mm (US 10) needles, cast on 138 sts.

BOTTOM WELT
Row 1 (RS): *K1, P1; rep from * to end of row.
Row 2: As row 1.
Rep rows 1 & 2 until bottom welt measures 12cm from cast on edge.

CABLE PATTERN
Beg and ending rows as indicated and repeating the 16 row patt repeat throughout, cont in patt from chart for 304 rows (19 patt repeats). Wrap should measure 138cm from start of cable pattern.

TOP WELT
Rep rows 1 & 2 until welt measures 12cm from start of welt. Cast off in rib.

MAKING UP
Press as described on the information page.
Sew in any loose ends on WS of wrap.

KEY

☐ K on RS, P on WS   C4B   C3B   C5B   C6B

• P on RS, K on WS   C4F   C3F   C5F   C6F

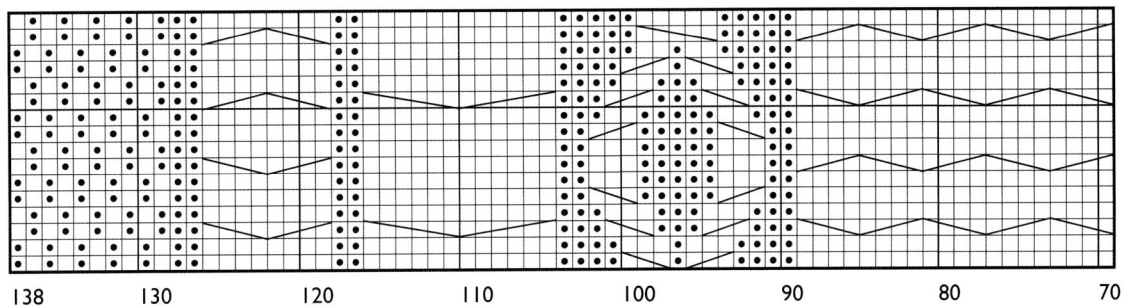

138   130   120   110   100   90   80   70

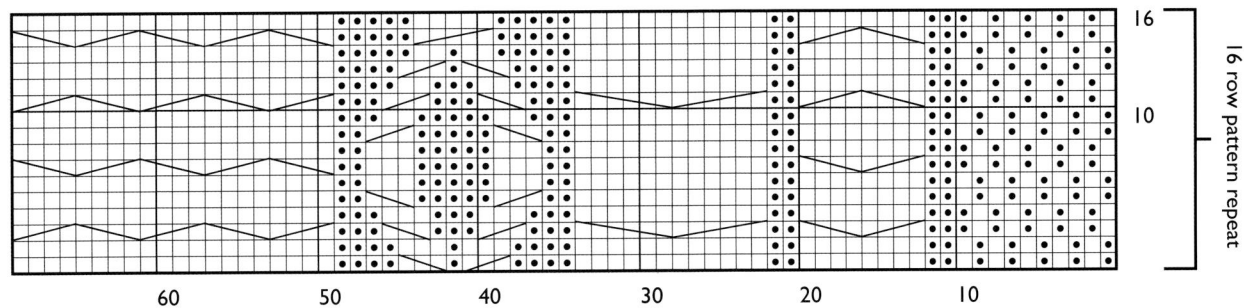

60   50   40   30   20   10

16

10

16 row pattern repeat

with a K round follows:

Rounds 1 – 104: Work the 52 round patt repeat twice using yarn B as main colour. Break off yarn B.
Rounds 105 – 208: Work the next two 52 round patt repeats using yarn C as main colour. Break off yarn C.
Rounds 209 – 312: Work the next two 52 round patt repeats using yarn D as main colour. Break off yarn D.
Rounds 313 – 416: Work the next two 52 round patt repeats using yarn E as the main colour. Break off yarn E.
Rounds 417 – 520: Work the next two 52 round patt repeats using yarn F as the main colour.

KEY

A ■ Seafarer 170

□ MAIN COLOUR
CHANGE COLOUR
EVERY 104 ROUNDS

B □ Watery 152

C □ Avocado 161

D □ Clay 177

E □ Cinnamon 175

F □ Ginger 154

MINT WRAP ●●●

One size only
Rowan Felted Tweed

A	Seafarer 170	7	× 50gm
B	Watery 152	2	× 50gm
C	Avocado 161	2	× 50gm
D	Clay 177	2	× 50gm
E	Cinnamon 175	2	× 50gm
F	Ginger 154	2	× 50gm

Needles
3¼mm (no 10) (US 3) circular needle

Tension
27 sts and 28.5 rounds to 10 cm measured over patterned st st using 3¼mm (US 3) needles.

Finished size
Completed wrap measures 38cm (15 ins) wide and 182cm (72 ins) long.

WRAP
Using 3¼mm (US 3) circular needles and yarn A cast on 208 sts.
Beg and ending rounds as indicated using **yarn A throughout** and using the **fairisle** technique as described on the information page, repeating the 52 st patt repeat 4 times across each round and the 52 round patt repeat throughout, cont in patt from chart which is worked entirely in st st beg

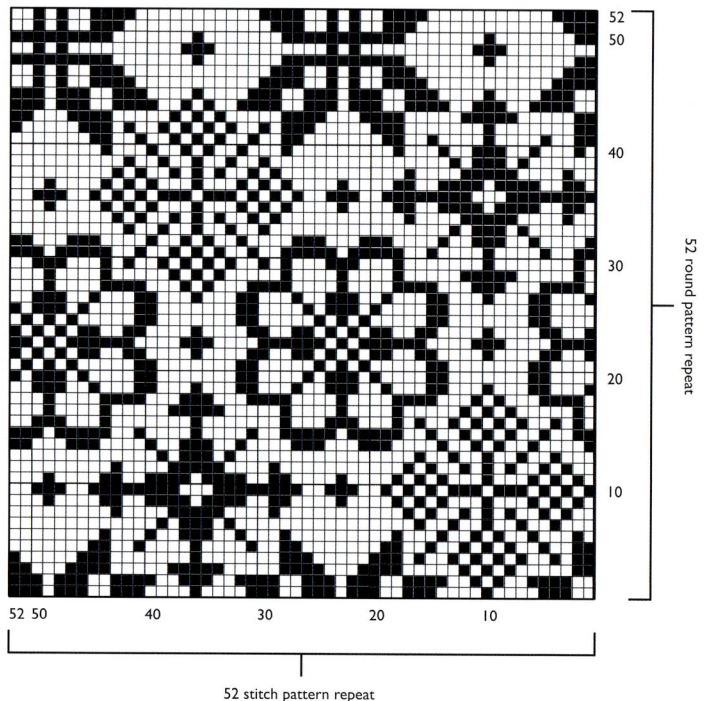

52 round pattern repeat

52 stitch pattern repeat

Cast off.

MAKING UP
Press as described on the information page.

COMFREY ●●●

	S	M	L	XL	XXL	
To fit bust	81-86	91-97	102-107	112-117	122-127	cm
	32-34	36-38	40-42	44-46	48-50	in

Rowan Cocoon

| | 12 | 12 | 13 | 13 | 14 | × 100gm |

(photographed in Frost 806)

Needles
1 pair 6mm (no 4) (US 10) needles
Cable needle
6.00mm (no 4) (US J10) crochet hook (optional)

Tension
15 sts and 20 rows to 10 cm measured over rev st st using 6mm (US 10) needles. Each body cable panel measures 14 cm wide.

Special abbreviations
C3F = slip next 2 sts onto cable needle and leave at front of work, K1 tbl,

slip centre (P) st of this group of 3 sts back onto left needle and P this st, then K1 tbl from cable needle; **C6B** = slip next 3 sts onto cable needle and leave at back of work, K3, then K3 from cable needle; **C6F** = slip next 3 sts onto cable needle and leave at front of work, K3, then K3 from cable needle; **Cr4L** = slip next 3 sts onto cable needle and leave at front of work, P1, then K3 from cable needle; **Cr4R** = slip next st onto cable needle and leave at back of work, K3, then P1 from cable needle; **Cr5L** = slip next 3 sts onto cable needle and leave at front of work, P2, then K3 from cable needle; **Cr5R** = slip next 2 sts onto cable needle and leave at back of work, K3, then P2 from cable needle; **Cr6L** = slip next 3 sts onto cable needle and leave at front of work, P3, then K3 from cable needle; **Cr6R** = slip next 3 sts onto cable needle and leave at back of work, K3, then P3 from cable needle.
See information page for US abbreviations.

Crochet abbreviations
ch = chain; **dc** = double crochet; **ss** = slip stitch.

BACK
Using 6mm (US 10) needles cast on 107 [115: 123: 133: 143] sts.
Row 1 (RS): P1 [0: 0: 2: 1], K3 [2: 0: 3: 3], *P3, K3, rep from * to last 1 [5: 3: 2: 1] sts, P1 [3: 3: 2: 1], K0 [2: 0: 0: 0].
Row 2: K1 [0: 0: 2: 1], P3 [2: 0: 3: 3], *K3, P3, rep from * to last 1 [5: 3: 2: 1] sts, K1 [3: 3: 2: 1], P0 [2: 0: 0: 0].

These 2 rows form rib.
Work in rib for a further 11 rows, ending with **WS** facing for next row.
Row 14 (WS): Rib 3 [4: 5: 7: 9], *(rib 1, M1, rib 1) 12 times*, rib 2 [4: 6: 8: 10], rep from * to * once more, rib 1 [2: 3: 4: 5], M1, rib 0 [1: 2: 3: 4], rep from * to * once more, rib 2 [4: 6: 8: 10], rep from * to * once more, rib 3 [4: 5: 7: 9]. 156 [164: 172: 182: 192] sts.
Now work in patt, placing cable panels, as folls:
Row 1 (RS): P3 [4: 5: 7: 9], *work next 36 sts as row 1 of body cable panel, P2 [4: 6: 8: 10], rep from * twice more, work next 36 sts as row 1 of body cable panel, P3 [4: 5: 7: 9].
Row 2: K3 [4: 5: 7: 9], *work next 36 sts as row 2 of body cable panel, K2 [4: 6: 8: 10], rep from * twice more, work next 36 sts as row 2 of body cable panel, K3 [4: 5: 7: 9].
These 2 rows set the sts – 4 cable panels with rev st st between and at sides.
Cont as now set until back meas 58 [60: 62: 64: 66] cm, ending with RS facing for next row.
Shape shoulders
Cast off all sts in patt, placing marker between centre 2 sts.

LEFT FRONT
Using 6mm (US 10) needles cast on 69 [73: 77: 82: 87] sts.

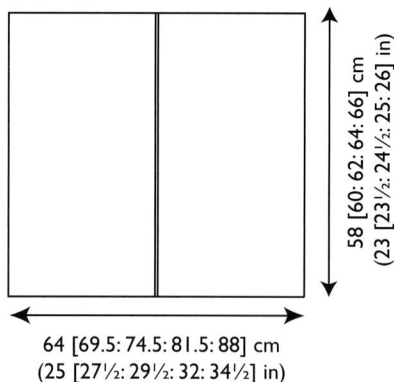

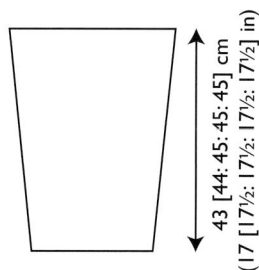

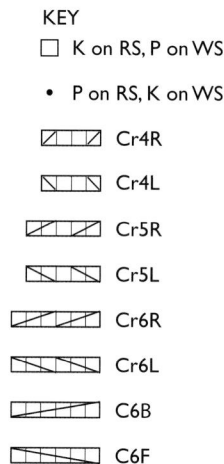

BODY CABLE PANEL

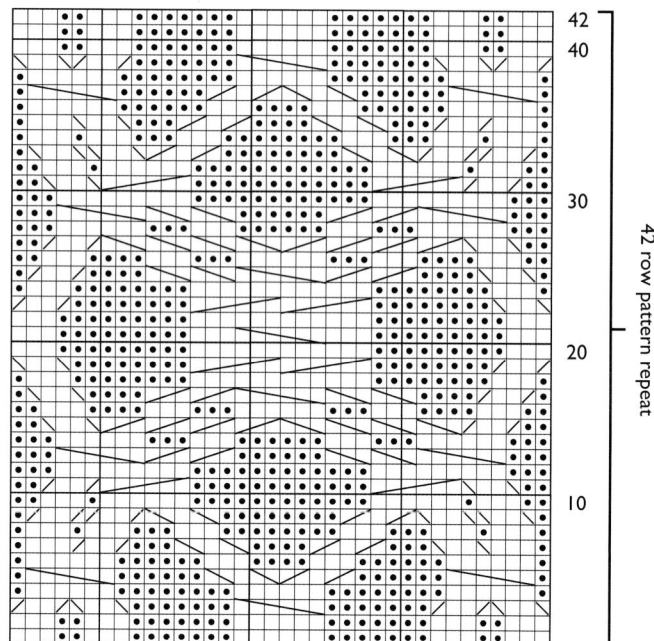

KEY

☐ K on RS, P on WS

• P on RS, K on WS

▱ Cr4R

▱ Cr4L

▱ Cr5R

▱ Cr5L

▱ Cr6R

▱ Cr6L

▱ C6B

▱ C6F

42 row pattern repeat

64 [69.5: 74.5: 81.5: 88] cm
(25 [27½: 29½: 32: 34½] in)

58 [60: 62: 64: 66] cm
(23 [23½: 24½: 25: 26] in)

43 [44: 45: 45: 45] cm
(17 [17½: 17½: 17½: 17½] in)

Row 1 (RS): P1 [0: 0: 2: 1], K3 [2: 0: 3: 3], *P3, K3, rep from * to last 17 sts, (P2, K1 tbl, P1, K1 tbl) 3 times, P1, K1.

Row 2: (K2, P1 tbl, K1, P1 tbl) 3 times, K2, P3, *K3, P3, rep from * to last 1 [5: 3: 2: 1] sts, K1 [3: 3: 2: 1], P0 [2: 0: 0: 0].

Row 3: P1 [0: 0: 2: 1], K3 [2: 0: 3: 3], *P3, K3, rep from * to last 17 sts, (P2, C3F) 3 times, P1, K1.

Row 4: As row 2.

These 4 rows set the sts – front opening edge 15 sts in cabled rib with all other sts in rib as given for back.

Cont as set for a further 9 rows, ending with **WS** facing for next row.

Row 14 (WS): Patt 15 sts, M1, rib 1 [2: 3: 4: 5], *(rib 1, M1, rib 1) 12 times*, rib 2 [4: 6: 8: 10], rep from * to * once more, rib 3 [4: 5: 7: 9]. 94 [98: 102: 107: 112] sts.

Now work in patt, placing cable panels, as folls:

Row 1 (RS): P3 [4: 5: 7: 9], work next 36 sts as row 1 of body cable panel, P2 [4: 6: 8: 10], work next 36 sts as row 1 of body cable panel, P2 [3: 4: 5: 6], patt 15 sts.

Row 2: Patt 15 sts, K2 [3: 4: 5: 6], work next 36 sts as row 2 of body cable panel, K2 [4: 6: 8: 10], work next 36 sts as row 2 of body cable panel, K3 [4: 5: 7: 9].

These 2 rows set the sts – front opening edge 15 sts still in cabled rib, and 2 cable panels with rev st st between and at sides.

Cont as now set until left front meas 58 [60: 62: 64: 66] cm, ending with RS facing for next row.

Shape shoulder

Cast off all sts in patt, placing marker 16 sts in from front opening edge – this marker should match to centre back marker.

RIGHT FRONT

Using 6mm (US 10) needles cast on 69 [73: 77: 82: 87] sts.

Row 1 (RS): K1, P1, (K1 tbl, P1, K1 tbl, P2) 3 times, K3, *P3, K3, rep from * to last 1 [5: 3: 2: 1] sts, P1 [3: 3: 2: 1], K0 [2: 0: 0: 0].

Row 2: K1 [0: 0: 2: 1], P3 [2: 0: 3: 3], *K3, P3, rep from * to last 17 sts, K2, (P1 tbl, K1, P1 tbl, K2) 3 times.

Row 3: K1, P1, (C3F, P2) 3 times, K3, *P3, K3, rep from * to last 1 [5: 3: 2: 1] sts, P1 [3: 3: 2: 1], K0 [2: 0: 0: 0].

Row 4: As row 2.

These 4 rows set the sts – front opening edge 15 sts in cabled rib with all other sts in rib as given for back.

Cont as set for a further 9 rows, ending with **WS** facing for next row.

Row 14 (WS): Rib 3 [4: 5: 7: 9], *(rib 1, M1, rib 1) 12 times*, rib 2 [4: 6: 8: 10], rep from * to * once more, rib 1 [2: 3: 4: 5], M1, patt 15 sts. 94 [98: 102: 107: 112] sts.

Now work in patt, placing cable panels, as folls:

Row 1 (RS): Patt 15 sts, P2 [3: 4: 5: 6], work next 36 sts as row 1 of body cable panel, P2 [4: 6: 8: 10], work next 36 sts as row 1 of body cable panel, P3 [4: 5: 7: 9].

Row 2: K3 [4: 5: 7: 9], work next 36 sts as row 2 of body cable panel,

SLEEVE CABLE PANEL

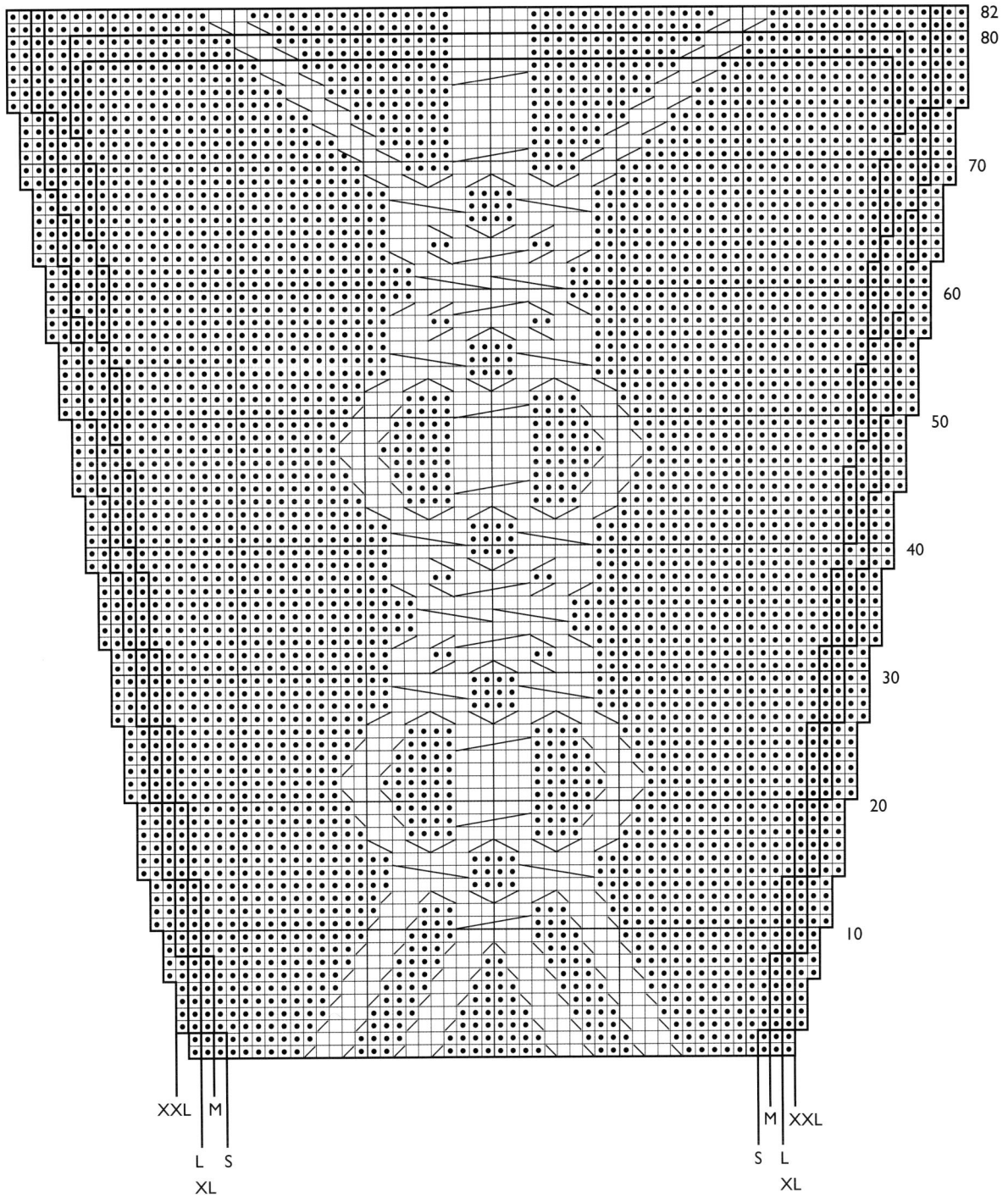

K2 [4: 6: 8: 10], work next 36 sts as row 2 of body cable panel, K2 [3: 4: 5: 6], patt 15 sts.
These 2 rows set the sts – front opening edge 15 sts still in cabled rib, and 2 cable panels with rev st st between and at sides.
Complete to match left front.

SLEEVES
Using 6mm (US 10) needles cast on 39 [41: 43: 43: 45] sts.
Row 1 (RS): P0 [1: 2: 2: 3], K3, *P3, K3, rep from * to last 0 [1: 2: 2: 3] sts, P0 [1: 2: 2: 3].
Row 2: K0 [1: 2: 2: 3], P3, *K3, P3, rep from * to last 0 [1: 2: 2: 3] sts, K0 [1: 2: 2: 3].
These 2 rows form rib.
Work in rib for a further 5 rows, ending with **WS** facing for next row.
Row 8 (WS): Rib 10 [11: 12: 12: 13], M1, rib 10, M1, rib 9, M1, rib 10 [11: 12: 12: 13]. 42 [44: 46: 46: 48] sts.
Beg and ending rows as indicated, now work in patt from chart for sleeve as folls:
Inc 1 st at each end of 3rd and 6 [5: 8: 12: 3] foll 6th [6th: 6th: 6th: 4th] rows, then on 4 [5: 3: -: 10] foll 8th [8th: 8th: -: 6th] rows, taking inc sts into rev st st. 64 [66: 70: 72: 76] sts.
Work 7 rows, ending with after chart row 78 [80: 82: 82: 82] and with RS facing for next row. (Sleeve should meas approx 43 [44: 45: 45: 45] cm.)
Cast off all sts in patt.

MAKING UP
Press as described on the information page.
Using back stitch, or mattress stitch if preferred, sew left shoulder seam from outer edge to markers. In same way, join right shoulder seam – shoulder seams meet at centre marker. Now join cast-off edges of front sections from front opening edge to markers – this seam forms centre back neck seam of grown-on front "bands" in cabled rib.
Mark points along side seam edges 20 [21: 22: 23: 24] cm either side of shoulder seams.
See information page for finishing instructions, setting in sleeves using the straight cast-off method.
Optional crochet trim
With RS facing and using 6.00mm (US J10) crochet hook, attach yarn at base of right front opening edge, 1 ch (does NOT count as st), now work 1 row of dc evenly up entire right front opening edge, then down entire left front opening edge, ensuring an odd number of dc is worked, turn.
Next row (WS): 1 ss into first dc, *3 ch, miss 1 dc, 1 ss into next dc, rep from * to end.
Fasten off.

L O V A G E ●●●

		S	M-L	L-XL	XXL	
To fit bust		81-86	91-107	107-117	122-127	cm
		32-34	36-42	42-46	48-50	in
Rowan Fine Tweed						
A	Arncliffe 360	8	9	10	11	x 25gm
B	Skipton 379	2	2	2	2	x 25gm
C	Richmond 381	2	2	2	2	x 25gm
D	Hawes 362	1	2	2	2	x 25gm
E	Leyburn 383	2	2	2	2	x 25gm
F	Tissington 386	1	1	1	1	x 25gm
G	Dove Dale 385	1	1	1	1	x 25gm
H	Dent 373	2	2	2	2	x 25gm
I	*Bedale 361	1	1	1	1	x 25gm

*Yarn I is used for optional crochet trim **only**

Needles
2¼mm (no 13) (US 1) circular needle
2¾mm (no 12) (US 2) circular needle
3¼mm (no 10) (US 3) circular needle
Set of 4 double-pointed 2¼mm (no 13) (US 1) needles
Set of 4 double-pointed 2¾mm (no 12) (US 2) needles
Set of 4 double-pointed 3¼mm (no 10) (US 3) needles
2.50mm (no 12) (US C2) crochet hook - optional

Tension
30 sts and 40 rows to 10 cm measured over plain st st using 2¾ mm (US 2) needles. 30 sts and 31 rows to 10 cm measured over patterned st st using 3¼ mm (US 3) needles.

Crochet abbreviations
ch = chain; **dc** = double crochet; **sp(s)** = space(s); **tr** = treble.
See information page for US abbreviations.

BODY (worked in one piece to armholes)
Using 2¼ mm (US 1) circular needle and yarn A cast on 264 [308: 352: 396] sts.
Taking care not to twist cast-on edge, work in rounds as folls:
Round 1 (RS): *K1, P1, rep from * to end.
This round forms rib.

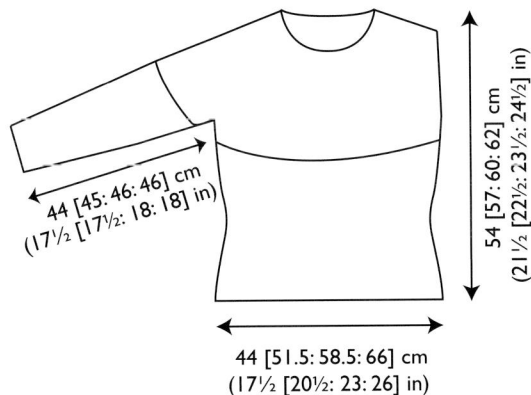

44 [45: 46: 46] cm
(17½ [17½: 18: 18] in)

54 [57: 60: 62] cm
(21½ [22½: 23½: 24½] in)

44 [51.5: 58.5: 66] cm
(17½ [20½: 23: 26] in)

Place marker between first and last sts of last round to denote beg and ends of rounds – this is centre back point.
Work in rib for a further 23 rounds.
Change to 2¾ mm (US 2) circular needle.
Next round (RS): Knit.
This round forms st st.
Work in st st for a further 1 [5: 9: 13] rounds.
Counting out from centre back marker/beg and ends of rounds, now place side seam markers as folls: miss 66 [77: 88: 99] sts either side of centre back and place a marker after last missed st – there should be 132 [154: 176: 198] sts between side seam markers at front and back.
Next round: *K to within 3 sts of side seam marker, K2tog, K2 (side seam marker is between these 2 sts), sl 1, K1, psso, rep from * once more, K to end. 260 [304: 348: 392] sts.
Working all side seam shaping as set by last round, dec 1 st at each side of both side seam markers on 6th [8th: 8th: 8th] and 0 [0: 2: 1] foll 8th rounds, then on 3 [3: 1: 2] foll 6th rounds. 244 [288: 332: 376] sts.
Work 9 [11: 11: 13] rounds.
Next round: *K to within 2 sts of side seam marker, M1, K4 (side seam marker is at centre of these 4 sts), M1, rep from * once more, K to end. 248 [292: 336: 380] sts.
Working all side seam increases as set by last round, inc 1 st at each side of both side seam markers on 4th and 3 foll 4th rounds.
264 [308: 352: 396] sts.
Work 1 round.
Change to 3¼ mm (US 3) circular needle.
Joining in and breaking off colours as required, using the **fairisle** technique as described on the information page and repeating the 44 st patt repeat 6 [7: 8: 9] times around each round, cont in patt from chart A, which is worked entirely in st st, as folls:

CHART B

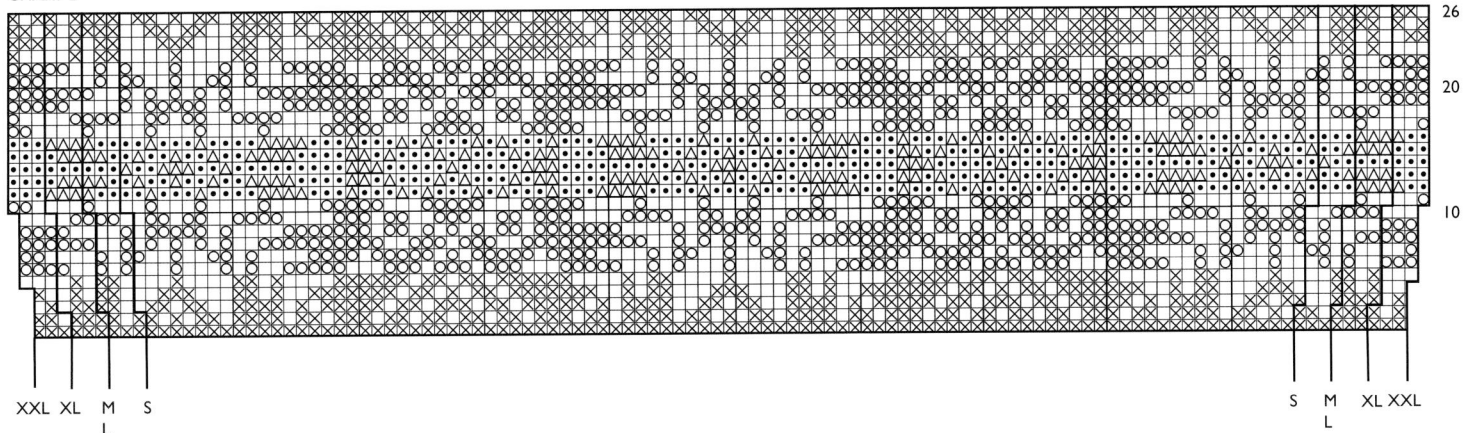

26
20
10

XXL XL M S
L

S M XL XXL
L

Work 26 rounds.
Divide for armholes
Next round: Using yarn B, K61 [72: 83: 94] and slip these sts onto a holder for left back, cast off next 10 sts (for left underarm), K until there are 122 [144: 166: 188] sts on right needle and slip these sts onto another holder for front, cast off next 10 sts (for right underarm), K to end and slip this last set of 61 [72: 83: 94] sts onto another holder for right back.
(Body should meas approx 28 [30: 32: 33] cm.)
Break yarn.

SLEEVES
Using set of 4 double-pointed 2¼mm (US 1) needles and yarn A cast on 58 [60: 64: 66] sts.
Taking care not to twist cast-on edge, work in rounds as folls:
Work in rib as given for body for 1 round.
Place marker between first and last sts of last round to denote beg and ends of rounds – this is underarm point.
Work in rib for a further 23 rounds.
Change to double-pointed 2¾mm (US 2) needles.
Work in st st for 4 [4: 4: 2] rounds.
Next round: K2, M1, K to last 2 sts, M1, K2.
Working all increases as set by last round, inc 1 st at each end of 6th [6th: 6th: 4th] and foll 9 [15: 17: 1] foll 6th [6th: 6th: 4th] rounds, then on 6 [2: 1: 19] foll 8th [8th: 8th: 6th] rounds. 92 [98: 104: 110] sts.
Work 5 [5: 5: 1] rounds.
Change to double-pointed 3¼mm (US 3) needles.
Beg and ending rows as indicated and joining in and breaking off colours as required, cont in patt from chart B, which is worked entirely in st st, as folls:
Inc 1 st at each end of 3rd [3rd: 3rd: 5th] and foll 8th [8th: 8th: 6th] round, taking inc sts into patt. 96 [102: 108: 114] sts.
Cont straight until chart row 26 has been completed.
Next round: Using yarn B, cast off 5 sts, K to last 5 sts, cast off rem 5 sts.
(Sleeve should meas 44 [45: 46: 46] cm.)
Break yarn and leave rem 86 [92: 98: 104] sts on a holder.

YOKE
With RS facing, using 3¼mm (US 3) circular needle and yarn F, work across sts on holders as folls: K across 61 [72: 83: 94] sts on left back holder dec 1 [1: 0: 1] st at centre, K across 86 [92: 98: 104] sts on left sleeve holder dec 2 [0: 0: 2] sts evenly, K across 122 [144: 166: 188] sts on front holder dec 2 [2: 0: 2] sts evenly, K across 86 [92: 98: 104] sts on right sleeve holder dec 2 [0: 0: 2] sts evenly, then K across 61 [72: 83: 94] sts on right back holder dec 1 [1: 0: 1] st at centre.
408 [468: 528: 576] sts.
Work 0 [0: 1: 2] rounds.
Joining in and breaking off colours as required and repeating the 12 st patt rep 34 [39: 44: 48] times around each round, cont in patt from chart C, which is worked entirely in st st, until all 38 rows of chart have been completed.
Next round: Using yarn G, *K2, K2tog, rep from * to end. 306 [351: 396: 432] sts.
(**Note:** As number of sts decreases, change from circular needle to set of 4 double-pointed needles).
Work 0 [1: 1: 2] rounds.
Joining in and breaking off colours as required and repeating the 9 st patt rep 34 [39: 44: 48] times around each round, cont in patt from chart D, which is worked entirely in st st, until all 20 rows of chart have been completed.
Next round: Using yarn B, *sl 1, K1, psso, K1, rep from * to end. 204 [234: 264: 288] sts.
Work 0 [1: 1: 2] rounds.
Joining in and breaking off colours as required and repeating the 6 st patt rep 34 [39: 44: 48] times around each round, cont in patt from chart E, which is worked entirely in st st, until all 20 rows of chart have been completed.
Break off all contrasts and cont using yarn A **only**.
Next round: *K2tog, K1, rep from * to end. 136 [156: 176: 192] sts.
Work 0 [0: 1: 2] rounds.
Change to double pointed 2¼mm (US 1) needles.
Work in rib as give for body for 6 rounds.
Cast off in rib.

MAKING UP
Press as described on the information page.
Join cast-off sts at underarms using back stitch, or mattress stitch if preferred.
Optional crochet trim (make 2)
Using 2.50mm (US C2) crochet hook and yarn I make 76 [80: 84: 84] ch.
Row 1 (RS): 1 tr into 6th ch from hook, *1 ch, miss 1 ch, 1 tr into next ch, rep from * to end, turn. 73 [77: 81: 81] sts, 36 [38: 40: 40] ch sps.
Row 2: 1 ch (does NOT count as st), 1 dc into tr at base of 1 ch, *5 ch, miss (1 ch, 1 tr and 1 ch), 1 dc into next tr, rep from * to end, working dc at end of last rep into next ch, turn. 18 [19: 20: 20] ch sps.
Row 3: 1 ch (does NOT count as st), 1 dc into dc at base of 1 ch, 7 dc into each ch sp to end, 1 dc into dc at beg of previous row, turn.
Row 4: 5 ch (counts as 1 tr and 2 ch), miss dc at base of 5 ch and next 3 dc, *1 dc into next dc, 3 ch, miss 6 dc, rep from * to last 5 dc, 1 dc into next dc, 2 ch, miss 3 dc, 1 tr into last dc, turn.
Row 5: 4 ch (counts as 1 tr and 1 ch), miss tr at base of 4 ch and next 2 ch, *1 tr into next dc, 1 ch**, 1 tr into next ch sp, 1 ch, rep from * to end, ending last rep at **, 1 tr into 3rd of 5 ch at beg of previous row.
Fasten off.
Using photograph as a guide, neatly sew trim in place along centre of sleeve, between top of rib and beg of chart B.
See information page for finishing instructions.

KEY

A □ Arncliffe 360

B ✕ Skipton 379

C ○ Richmond 381

D • Hawes 362

E ■ Leyburn 383

F ◤ Tissington 386

G | Dove Dale 385

H △ Dent 373

CHART A

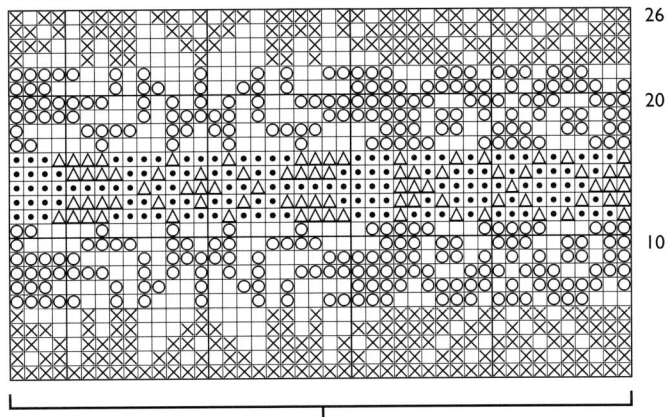

44 stitch pattern repeat

CHART C

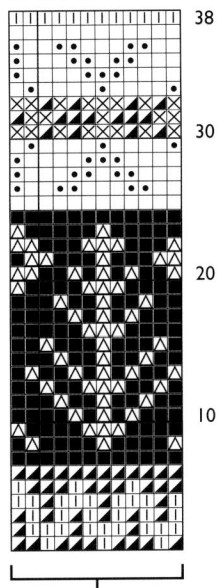

12 stitch pattern repeat

CHART D

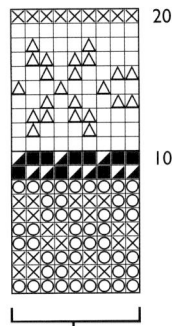

9 stitch pattern repeat

CHART E

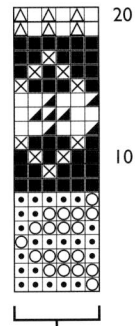

6 stitch pattern repeat

W I L L O W ●●

	S	M	L	XL	XXL	
To fit bust	81-86	91-97	102-107	112-117	122-127	cm
	32-34	36-38	40-42	44-46	48-50	in

Rowan Felted Tweed Aran

		S	M	L	XL	XXL	
A	Garden 740	8	9	10	10	11	x 50gm
B	Mahogany 734	1	1	1	1	1	x 50gm
C	Cork 721	2	2	2	2	2	x 50gm
D	Pebble 720	1	1	2	2	2	x 50gm

Needles

1 pair 4mm (no 8) (US 6) needles
1 pair 4½mm (no 7) (US 7) needles
1 pair 5mm (no 6) (US 8) needles
4mm (no 8) (US 6) circular needle

Tension

18½ sts and 24 rows to 10 cm measured over plain st st using 4½mm
(US 7) needles. 18½ sts and 18½ rows to 10 cm measured over
patterned st st using 5mm (US 8) needles.

BACK

Using 4mm (US 6) needles and yarn A cast on 96 [104: 120: 132: 148] sts.
Row 1 (RS): K3, *P2, K2, rep from * to last st, K1.
Row 2: K1, P2, *K2, P2, rep from * to last st, K1.
These 2 rows form rib.

Work in rib for a further 11 rows, ending with **WS** facing for next row.
Row 14 (WS): Rib 5 [6: 4: 5: 3], work 2 tog, (rib 12 [13: 9: 8: 8], work
2 tog) 6 [6: 10: 12: 14] times, rib 5 [6: 4: 5: 3].
89 [97: 109: 119: 133] sts.
Change to 4½mm (US 7) needles.
Beg with a K row, work in st st until back meas 12 cm, ending with RS
facing for next row.
Cast on 6 sts at beg of next 2 rows. 101 [109: 121: 131: 145] sts.
Work 2 rows, ending with RS facing for next row.
Change to 5mm (US 8) needles.
Using the **fairisle** technique as described on the information page, joining
in and breaking off colours as required and beg and ending rows as
indicated, cont in patt from chart A, which is worked entirely in st st beg
with a K row, as folls:
Work 2 rows.
Dec 1 st at each end of next row. 99 [107: 119: 129: 143] sts.
Work 14 rows, ending after chart row 17. First band of patt completed.
Break off contrasts and cont using yarn A **only**.
Change to 4½mm (US 7) needles.
Beg with a P row, work in st st for 17 [17: 19: 19: 21] rows, dec 1 st at
each end of 2nd of these rows and ending with RS facing for next row.
97 [105: 117: 127: 141] sts.
Change to 5mm (US 8) needles.
Using the **fairisle** technique as described on the information page, joining
in and breaking off colours as required and beg and ending rows as
indicated, cont in patt from chart B, which is worked entirely in st st beg
with a K row, as folls:
Dec 1 st at each end of next row. 95 [103: 115: 125: 139] sts.
Work 17 rows, ending after chart row 18. Second band of patt
completed.
Break off contrasts and cont using yarn A **only**.
Change to 4½mm (US 7) needles.
Beg with a K row, work in st st for 20 [20: 22: 22: 24] rows, dec 1 st at
each end of first of these rows and ending with RS facing for next row.

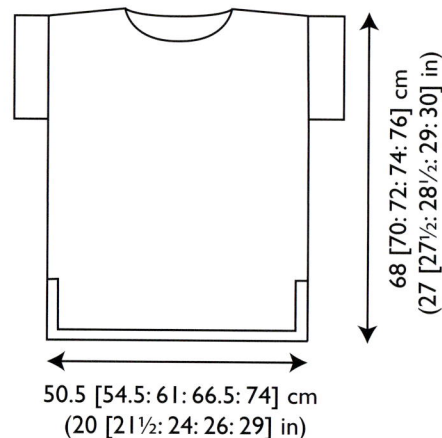

68 [70: 72: 74: 76] cm
(27 [27½: 28½: 29: 30] in)

50.5 [54.5: 61: 66.5: 74] cm
(20 [21½: 24: 26: 29] in)

93 [101: 113: 123: 137] sts.
Change to 5mm (US 8) needles.
Using the **fairisle** technique as described on the information page, joining in and breaking off colours as required and beg ending rows as indicated, cont in patt from chart C, which is worked entirely in st st beg with a K row, as folls:
Work 24 rows, ending after chart row 24. Third band of patt completed.
Break off contrasts and cont using yarn A **only**.
Change to 4½mm (US 7) needles.
Beg with a K row, complete back in st st as folls:
Cont straight until back meas 62 [64: 66: 68: 70] cm, ending with RS facing for next row.

Shape shoulders
Cast off 3 [4: 4: 5: 6] sts at beg of next 6 rows, then 3 [4: 5: 5: 6] sts at beg of foll 2 rows. 69 [69: 79: 83: 89] sts.

Shape back neck
Next row (RS): Cast off 4 [4: 5: 5: 6] sts, K until there are 16 [16: 19: 21: 22] sts on right needle and turn, leaving rem sts on a holder.
Work each side of neck separately.
Dec 1 st at neck edge of next 4 rows **and at same time** cast off 4 [4: 5: 5: 6] sts at beg of 2nd row, then 4 [4: 5: 6: 6] sts at beg of foll alt row.
Work 1 row.
Cast off rem 4 [4: 5: 6: 6] sts.
With RS facing, slip centre 29 [29: 31: 31: 33] sts onto a holder, rejoin yarn and K to end.
Complete to match first side, reversing shapings.

FRONT
Work as given for back until 0 [0: 2: 2: 4] rows less have been worked than on back to beg of shoulder shaping, ending with RS facing for next row.

Sizes S and M only
Shape shoulder and front neck
Next row (RS): Cast off 3 [4: -: -: -] sts, K until there are 33 [36: -: -: -] sts on right needle and turn, leaving rem sts on a holder.
Work each side of neck separately.
Cast off 3 [4: -: -: -] sts at beg of 2nd and foll 2 alt rows, then 4 sts at beg of foll 3 alt rows **and at same time** dec 1 st at neck edge of next 6 rows, then on 2 foll alt rows.

Sizes L, XL and XXL only
Shape front neck
Next row (RS): K- [-: 46: 51: 58] and turn, leaving rem sts on a holder.
Work each side of neck separately.
Dec 1 st at neck edge of next – [-: 1: 1: 3] rows, ending with RS facing

for next row. – [-: 45: 50: 55] sts.
Shape shoulder
Cast off – [-: 4: 5: 6] sts at beg of next and foll – [-: 2: 5: 6] alt rows, then – [-: 5: 6: -] sts at beg of foll – [-: 4: 1: -] alt rows **and at same time** dec 1 st at neck edge of next – [-: 5: 5: 3] rows, then on – [-: 3: 3: 4] foll alt rows.
All sizes
Work 1 row.
Cast off rem 4 [4: 5: 6: 6] sts.
With RS facing, slip centre 21 sts onto a holder, rejoin yarn and K to end.
Complete to match first side, reversing shapings.

MAKING UP
Press as described on the information page.
Join both shoulder seams using back stitch, or mattress stitch if preferred.
Collar
With RS facing, using 4mm (US 6) circular needle and yarn A, pick up and knit 15 [15: 18: 18: 19] sts down left side of front neck, K across 21 sts on front holder inc 2 sts evenly, pick up and knit 15 [15: 18: 18: 19] sts up right side of front neck, and 6 sts down right side of back neck, K across 29 [29: 31: 31: 33] sts on back holder inc 2 sts evenly, then pick up and knit 6 sts up left side of back neck. 96 [96: 104: 104: 108] sts.
Round 1: *K2, P2, rep from * to end.
Rep this round until collar meas 18 cm.
Cast off **loosely** in rib.
Armhole borders (both alike)
Mark points along side seam edges 24 [25: 26: 27: 28] cm either side of shoulder seams.
With RS facing, using 4mm (US 6) needles and yarn A, pick up and knit 96 [100: 104: 108: 112] sts evenly along armhole opening edges between marked points.
Beg with row 2, work in rib as given for back for 6 cm, ending with RS facing for next row.
Cast off in rib.
Side opening borders (all 4 alike)
With RS facing, using 4mm (US 6) needles and yarn A, pick up and knit 24 sts evenly along row-end edge of side openings, between original cast-on edge and sts cast on at top of openings.
Beg with row 2, work in rib as given for back for 7 rows, ending with RS facing for next row.
Cast off in rib.
Neatly sew one row-end edge of each border to cast-on sts at top of openings.
See information page for finishing instructions, leaving side seams open along side opening borders.

KEY

☐ A. Garden 740

○ B. Mahogany 734

■ C. Cork 721

✕ D. Pebble 720

CHART A

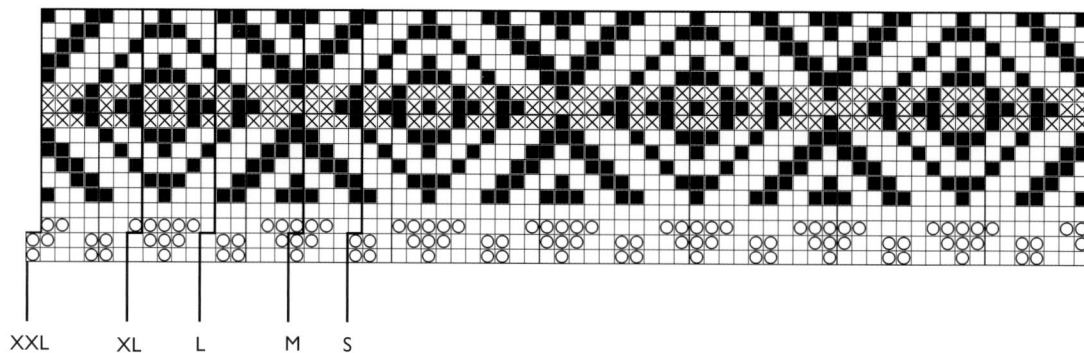

XXL   XL   L   M   S

CHART B

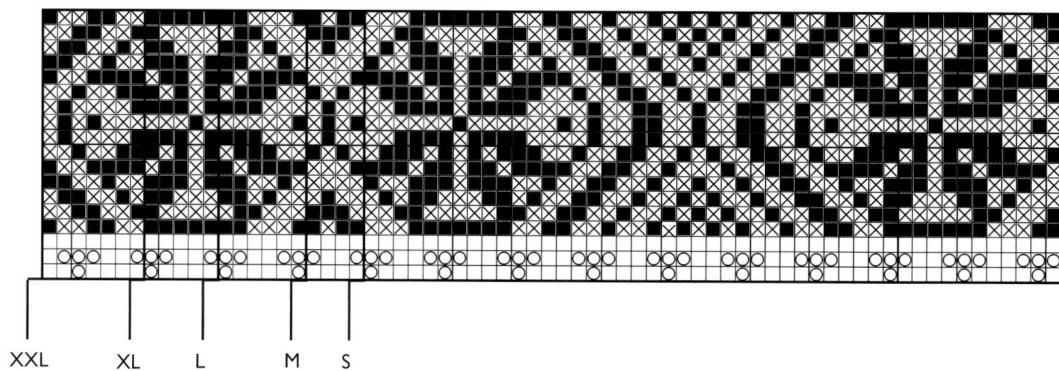

XXL   XL   L   M   S

CHART C

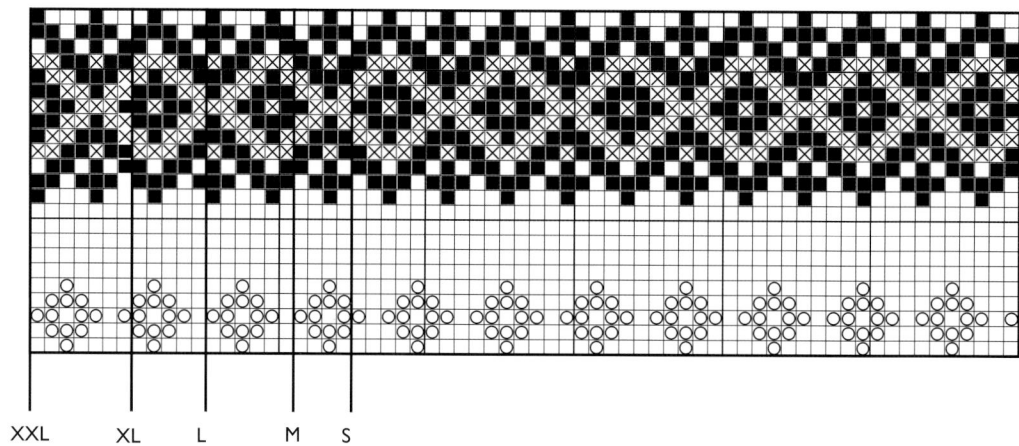

XXL   XL   L   M   S

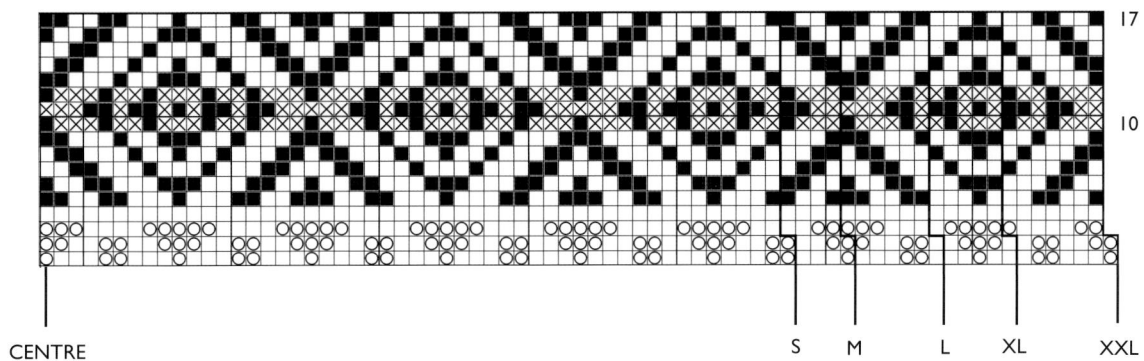

CENTRE   S   M   L   XL   XXL

17

10

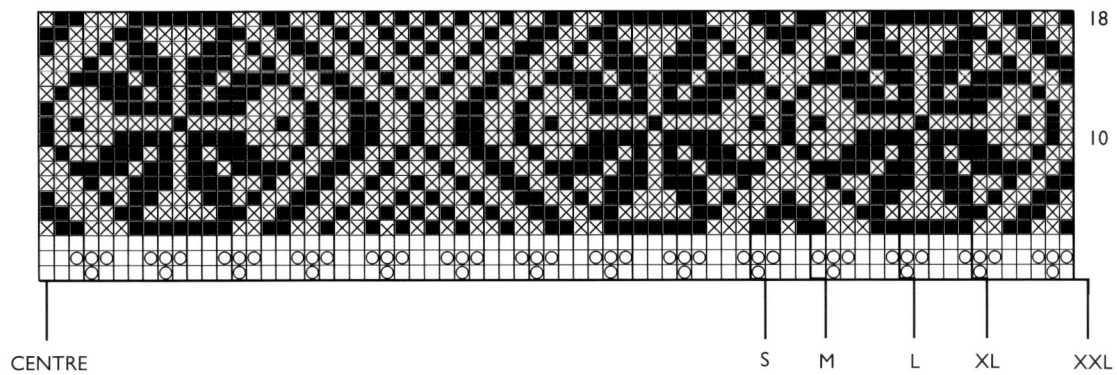

CENTRE   S   M   L   XL   XXL

18

10

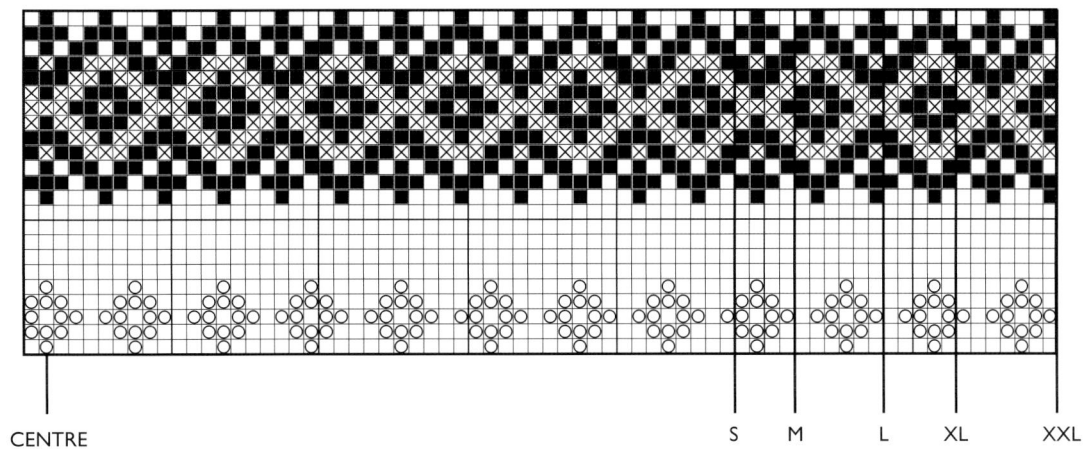

CENTRE   S   M   L   XL   XXL

71

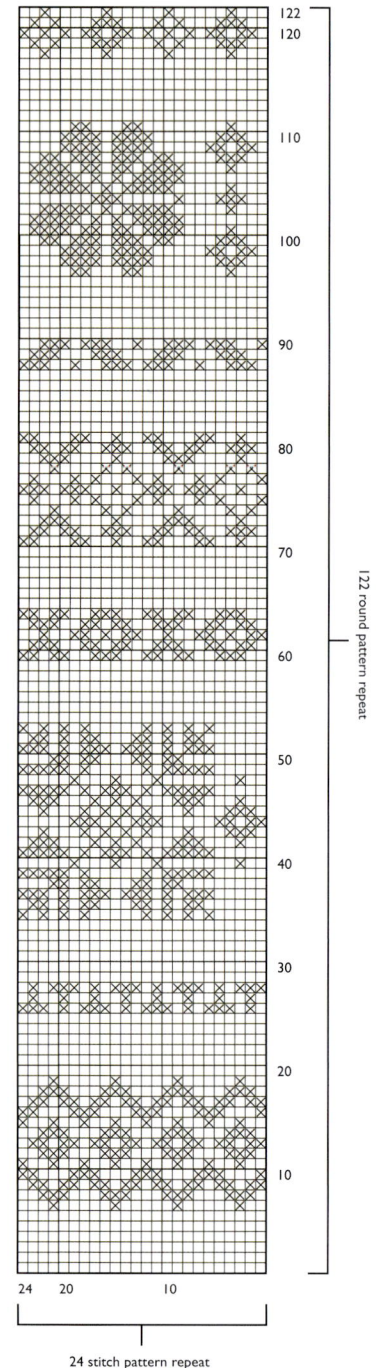

Sew in any loose ends on WS of scarf.
Smooth out the scarf so that it is flat and close the bottom edges together and the top edges together using mattress stitch.

O A K   S C A R F ●●●

One size only
Rowan Felted Tweed
A Peony 183   7   x 50gm
B Frozen 185   5   x 50gm

Needles
3¼mm (no 10) (US 3) circular needle

Tension
27 sts and 28.5 rounds to 10 cm measured over patterned st st using 3¼mm (US 3) needles.

Finished size
Completed scarf measures 35.5cm (14 ins) wide and 171cm (67 ins) long.

SCARF
Using 3¼mm (US 3) circular needles and yarn A cast on 192 sts.
Beg and ending rounds as indicated, using **yarn A & B throughout** and using the **fairisle** technique as described on the information page, repeating the 24 st patt repeat 8 times across each round and the 122 round patt repeat throughout, cont in patt from chart which is worked entirely in st st beg with a K round for 488 rounds (4 repeats).
Cast off.

MAKING UP
Press as described on the information page.

KEY

A ☐ Peony 183

B ✕ Frozen 185

122 round pattern repeat

24 stitch pattern repeat

TENSION

Achieving the correct tension is one of the most important factors when knitting one of my designs. I cannot stress highly enough that you really do need to knit a tension square BEFORE you start to knit the garment. The tension stated on each of my patterns must be achieved to ensure that the garment fits correctly and that it matches the measurements stated on the size diagram. I recommend that you knit a square using the number of stitches and rows stated on the pattern tension plus 3 or 4 stitches and rows. To check your tension, place the knitted square on a flat surface and mark out a 10cm square using pins as markers. Count the number of stitches and rows between the pins. If you have too many stitches, then your knitting is too tight, knit another square using a thicker needle. If you have too few stitches, then your knitting is too loose, knit another square using a thinner needle. It is also important to keep checking your tension whilst you are knitting your garment especially if you are returning to knit after leaving your work for a period of time.

SIZING

The patterns are written giving the instructions for the smallest size, for the other sizes work the figures in the brackets. The measurements stated on the size diagrams are the measurements of your finished garment AFTER pressing.

MODEL SIZE

Georgia is 5' 8" tall and is a standard size 8/10 and she is wearing the smallest size in each photograph.

CHARTS

Most of my patterns use a chart. Each square on the chart represents one stitch and each line of squares represents one row of knitting. When working from a chart odd rows (RS) read from right to left and even rows (WS) from left to right. Each chart has a key which either states the colours to be used or the stitches to be used.

COLOURWORK

Fairisle and Intarsia are the two main methods of adding colour into knitting.

Fairisle is used when two or three colours are to be worked repeatedly along a row. The colour not being used is stranded fairly loosely behind the stitches being worked. It is very important not to pull this stranded yarn too tight as this will pucker your knitting and your stitch tension will be too tight, make sure to spread your stitches to ensure that they remain elastic. I would recommend that you carry the stranded or floating yarn over no more than 5 stitches when using a DK or 4 Ply yarn, and no

more than 3 stitches when using an Aran or Chunky yarn. Weave the stranded colour under and over the colour being worked if you have to knit a colour over more than the recommended amount.

Intarsia creates a single thickness of knitting and is used when a colour is only required in a particular part of a row and does not form a repeating pattern. It can also be used in fairisle knitting when adding a third or fourth colour where weaving in stranded colours will be too much. The easiest method of working intarsia is to cut short lengths of yarn for each motif or colour block used in a row. Join in the colour at the appropriate part of the row according to the chart linking one colour to the next by twisting them around each other where they meet on the wrong side of the knitting to avoid any gaps. If your yarns get tangled then simply pull the short length through the tangle. All the ends can be either sewn in or more ideally woven in along the row as the colour is being knitted, this is done using the same method of weaving colours in fairisle knitting.

FINISHING

Finishing your garment beautifully is another important factor when making one of my designs. Good finishing will ensure that your garment fits correctly and washes and wears well. I urge you to spend time pressing and stitching your garment together, after all you've just spent a lot money and time knitting it using lovely Rowan yarns and the last thing you want to do is ruin it with bad finishing!

PRESSING

Firstly sew in any loose ends to the wrong side of the knitting. Block out each piece of knitting and then press according to the care instructions stated on the yarn ball bands. Always press using an iron on the wrong side of the knitting over a protective cloth (this can be damp or dry) and have the steam setting switched on the iron. Pay particular attention to the sides or edges of each piece as this will make the sewing up both easier and neater. Take special care with the welts and cuffs of the knitting – if the garment is fitted then gently steam the ribs so that they fill out but remain elastic. If the garment is a boxy, straight shape then steam press out the ribs to correct width.

STITCHING

When stitching the pieces together, remember to match areas of colour, texture or pattern very carefully where they meet. I recommend that you use mattress stitch wherever possible, this stitch gives the neatest finish ensuring that the seam lays flat.

Having knitted your pieces according to the pattern instructions, generally the shoulder seams of the front and back are now joined together using mattress stitch. Work the neck trim according to the pattern instructions and then join the neckband seams using mattress stitch if required. Knit neck bands or collars to the length stated in the pattern instructions, slightly stretching the trims before measuring if knitted in garter stitch or horizontal ribbing. Please take extra care when stitching the edgings and collars around the neck of the garment as these control the stretch of the neck. The sleeves are now normally added to the garment, take care to match the centre of the sleeve head to the shoulder seam. Ideally stretch the sleeve head into the armhole and stitch in place, if the sleeve head is too large for the armhole then check your tension as your knitting may be too loose. Join the underarm and side seams. Slip stitch any pockets or pocket lining into place and sew on buttons corresponding to the button holes lining up the outside edge of the button with the edging join or seam.

Carefully press your finished garment again to the measurements stated on the size diagram.

AFTERCARE
Ensure that you wash and dry your garment according to the care instructions stated on the yarn ball bands. If your garment uses more than one type of yarn then wash according to the most delicate. Reshape your garment when slightly damp and then carefully press to size again.

BUTTONS
The buttons used on the garments in this collection were from various sources. I recommend that you contact Bedecked Haberdashery to find similar buttons:

Bedecked Haberdashery,
Willow Cottage Workshop,
New Radnor,
Presteigne,
Powys LD8 2SS
Tel: +44 (0)1544 350577
Email: the_girls@bedecked.co.uk
Web: www.bedecked.co.uk

EXPERIENCE RATING
For guidance only.

● suitable for a beginner knitter with a little experience.

● ● suitable for a knitter with average ability.

● ● ● suitable for the experienced knitter.

CROCHET ABBREVIATIONS
The crochet patterns are written in the English style, however I am aware that the terminology varies from country to country. To help you, listed below are the English abbreviations with the US alternatives.

ENGLISH		US	
ch	chain	ch	chain
dc	double crochet	sc	single crochet
htr	half treble	hdc	half double crochet
tr	treble	dc	double crochet
dtr	double treble	tr	treble

KNITTING ABBREVIATIONS

K	knit
P	purl
st(s)	stitch(es)
inc	increas(e)(ing)
dec	decreas(e)(ing)
st st	stocking stitch (1 row K, 1 row P)
g st	garter stitch (K every row)
beg	begin(ning)
foll	following
rem	remain(ing)
rev st st	reverse stocking stitch (1 row K, 1 row P)
rep	repeat
alt	alternate
cont	continue
patt	pattern
tog	together
mm	millimetres
cm	centimetres
in(s)	inch(es)
RS	right side
WS	wrong side
sl 1	slip one stitch
psso	pass slip stitch over
p2sso	pass 2 slipped stitches over
tbl	through back of loop
M1	make one stitch by picking up the horizontal loop before the next stitch and knitting into the back of it
M1P	make one stitch by picking up the horizontal loop before the next stitch and purling into the back of it
yfwd	yarn forward
yrn	yarn round needle
meas	measures
0	no stitches, times or rows
-	no stitches, times or rows for that size
yon	yarn over needle
yfrn	yarn forward round needle
wyib	with yarn at back